CHEL...
is our name

Also available from Boxtree:

CHELSEA
is our name

A Collection of Fans' Tributes, Memories and Stories of Chelsea Football Club

Edited by Mark Hillsdon

B⧈XTREE

First published in 1999 by Boxtree, an imprint of
Macmillan Publishers Ltd, 25 Eccleston Place, London, SW1W 9NF
and Basingstoke

Associated companies throughout the world

ISBN 0 7522 2463 8

9 8 7 6 5 4 3 2 1

A CIP catalogue record for this book is available from
the British Library

Typeset by SX Composing DTP, Rayleigh, Essex
Printed by Mackays of Chatham Plc

Contents

Acknowledgements

Many thanks to Giles Smith, John Motson, Mark Hillsdon, and Adam Porter for writing pieces for this book, and to Tony Banks, Eric Bristow, Andy Cairns, Barbara Charone, Roddy Doyle, Andy Fletcher, Derek Fowlds, Andy Hamilton, Paul Hardcastle, Clive Mantle, David Mellor, Brian Moore, Pat Nevin, Paul Oakenfold, Peter Osgood, Lance Percival, Steven Redgrave, Francis Wheen and Jimmy White for agreeing to be interviewed for it.

The Contributors

Tony Banks

His experiences and memories as an MP, Minister for Sport and member of the GLC pale into insignificance compared to his recollections of Chelsea's 1954–55 Championship season.

Eric Bristow

The man who helped drag darts out of the tap room and on to the telly. A self-confessed armchair supporter, the Crafty Cockney now lives in Stoke and counts Sir Stanley Matthews among his friends.

Andy Cairns

Front man with rock band Therapy?, who first came across Chelsea when he discovered his father and his uncles ensconced in front of the telly watching the 1970 FA Cup final – along with a crate or two of beer.

Barbara Charone

The only female, American, ex-music journalist to support Chelsea. Barbara is Director of Publicity at WEA Records and threw a party the day John Hollins was sacked.

Roddy Doyle

Award-winning author who remains baffled as to why Chelsea are linked to Linfield and Rangers and why on earth his son has decided to support Liverpool.

Chelsea is our name

Andy Fletcher

One of the three surviving members of eighties' pop sensations Depeche Mode, who loved Pat Nevin until he slagged the band off in the music press. Claims to have learnt his ABC reading the half-time scores at the Bridge.

Derek Fowlds

Mr Derek, as Basil Brush once affectionately knew him, continues to star in *Heartbeat* and is a member of the infamous BBC Chelsea Drama Mafia. Confesses to sneaking his son through the turnstiles without paying.

Andy Hamilton

Another award-winning writer, responsible for, among other things, *Drop the Dead Donkey*. Andy hankers after the days when 'Strolling' echoed round Stamford Bridge.

Paul Hardcastle

Singer/songwriter who made a small fortune from the number '19' back in the 1980s. Still big in America and writing incidental music for Chelsea TV, Paul has never got to grips with 'One Man Went To Mow'.

Mark Hillsdon

Freelance journalist who cut his teeth writing rugby league reports for the *Salford City Reporter*. Has since written about serious sport for the *Chelsea* magazine, *FC* and *Football Monthly*. Admits to briefly calling his dog Osgood just so he could shout, 'Osgood is good'.

Clive Mantle

Actor and former star of the hit TV series *Casualty*, Clive is now back in an altogether different theatre, treading the boards up and down the country. Used to criticize Graham

Wilkins in hushed tones in case brother Ray heard and left the club.

David Mellor

The voice of *606*, head of the Football Taskforce and one of the few men to ever try and unfurl an umbrella in the Shed.

Brian Moore

The most capped British hooker ever, Brian played sixty-four times for England and was an inspirational leader of the pack. Now a solicitor working in London, he thinks Dennis Wise would have made a great scrum-half.

John Motson

At last the man whose encyclopaedic football memory has enthralled us for years comes clean about which colours he wears on the sleeve of that famous sheepskin coat, with recollections of a young firebrand called James Greaves.

Pat Nevin

Socialite, indie pop fan and second only to Charlie Cooke when it comes to tricky little Scots buggers jinking down the wing. Once risked the wrath of the Goodison Park faithfull to support Chelsea. Now player/chief executive at Motherwell.

Paul Oakenfold

Leading club DJ and record producer, whose recent work includes England's World Cup song. Dedicated to the cause from an early age, Paul's first Chelsea away game took him to exotic Hereford.

Peter Osgood

Chelsea hero. 150 goals in 375 games. Enough said.

Chelsea is our name

Lance Percival

Star of *Carry On* fame and films of a similar ilk, Lance was an incurable romantic who regularly took first dates to Stamford Bridge. Now a successful speaker on the after-dinner circuit.

Adam Porter

Journalist and idiot Adam Porter recently acquired the autograph of Steve Finnieston, now a building rep, his first Chelsea hero. Porter ghosts Stamford's column in *Onside*.

Steven Redgrave

The man who refuses to retire is now aiming for a record-breaking fifth consecutive Olympic gold medal in Sydney, this time in the coxless fours. If he ever needed one, would opt for Zola as his cox.

Giles Smith

Journalist and author who can regularly be seen sitting in the Matthew Harding stand pinching himself just in case it all really is a dream.

Francis Wheen

Private Eye and *Guardian* writer Francis learned all he knows about writing from *Shoot!* and believes that Ian Hutchinson and his long throws have never received the credit they deserve.

Jimmy White

Snooker enigma and five-times runner-up in the World Championship. Everything that Steve Davis isn't. Tries to be inconspicuous at games, even when he's got John Virgo at his side.

Tony Banks

Back in the early fifties, my dad used to take me to see a few clubs such as Charlton, Crystal Palace and even Millwall occasionally. Millwall had a reputation for being a real tough dockers' club and I think they wanted to live up to it. It was a fearsome place to go to. But Chelsea was the club that I got hooked on and I've been with them ever since. Fortunately my interest was sufficiently worked up to be really in the swing of things for the 1954–55 season and you couldn't really have chosen a better season to have as your first full one at Stamford Bridge. I managed to see every single home match and I still re-read the programmes to this day.

All in all I've been a pretty lucky supporter because in the ninety-four years that Chelsea have been in existence, I've seen most of their great triumphs. Those who supported Chelsea for the first fifty years may have seen us winning the

Championship at the very end of that period, but until then it was a very empty cupboard. And then, of course, there wasn't much to celebrate for a long time after that.

Supporting Chelsea was a big thing at school. My school was in Kennington, near the Oval, and Arsenal and Chelsea were the predominant teams – there were some Millwall and Charlton supporters too. We used to split up into our own little supporters' clubs and collect money. I can't really remember why but I'm sure it had something to do with smoking cheap cigarettes and eating lots of bread pudding.

I can't remember who had the most supporters but I know there was a lot of feeling between Arsenal and Chelsea. Don't forget, Arsenal were the Manchester United of those days. They were the big successful team. They had the Comptons, their marble halls and their busts and you used to think what stuck-up bastards they were. You used to hate them. Mind you, I do actually look forward to the day when other fans start singing 'Stand up if you hate Chelsea' because then I know we will have reached a level of success. They'll be singing out of sheer and utter jealousy, and I want them to be jealous of us.

I tended to go to Stamford Bridge on my own. I picked up the bug very early. To be honest, I didn't need anyone to go with. As soon I was old enough, I went. I knew all the people around me and I knew exactly where I stood at every single game. I went to the exact same spot. I used to negotiate myself into position by looking at the faces and just snuggling in. I knew all the faces but never any of the names. Two inches to the left or two inches to the right, and it was wrong. I had to be exactly 'there'. It was just to the right of the goal in the North End (now the Matthew Harding Stand).

In those days Stamford Bridge was a huge ground. It was largely uncovered and you got soaking wet if it rained and half died of the cold. But, as for so many supporters, Stamford Bridge was a big part of the attraction of supporting Chelsea. I used to go to reserve matches as well and I remember one bloody game, I was virtually the only person on the terraces. I could have sat in the stands, but I wasn't interested. I still had to go to my regular position! It was an icy winter's afternoon and by the time the match had finished my feet were so cold they were dead. I couldn't move. So I actually had to get on my hands and knees and start crawling out of the ground. I got into a bit of a panic because I convinced myself I was going to get locked in because I was completely on my own. I obviously made it out in the end though.

As well as the ground itself, the merchandising has changed beyond recognition. The only souvenir you could get when I started supporting them was a badge! Now, when you think of the merchandising, Christ, I would have died in heaven if I could have got my hands on what they've got today. In the fifties, you wanted any little souvenir with the Chelsea logo on, but there wasn't much. A badge, a mug if I remember rightly, and a blazer badge if you were in the supporters' club – that was it. There was nothing, yet you were desperate for some little thing that you could hold on to because it was your club.

I joined the supporters' club mainly to go on the away trips. Of course, the away following in those days wasn't as substantial as it is now because it used to take a hell of a long time to get to some of those places. Even Birmingham on the train could take as much as five hours. Travelling time only really came down in the sixties when they built the M1. So to watch them play in Newcastle you'd go up on the train overnight and it cost a lot. I couldn't afford to go away all the time. I used to save myself for FA Cup matches.

My dad's family all came from Birmingham, so when we played up there we used to make a special trip. We'd see Birmingham or someone like that and we'd all troop to St Andrews and stand with my dad's family. We used to have great fun.

That was in the days of reverse fixtures on Christmas Day and Boxing Day. I used to love going to football on Boxing Day. I think they tried to arrange those games as local derbies to minimize the travel. Going to football in those days was part of the Christmas tradition. You used to go out with the old

man and meet up with his mates and everyone was
smoking little Wills Wiffs and seemed to be wearing
new yellow gloves. It was Christmas, after all, and
we were celebrating. Don't forget, these were real
down-to-earth, working-class families, and tradition
was important.

Most of the games that stand out were during
that Championship year. The most vivid, if only
because of one particular event, was the match
against Wolverhampton Wanderers in April 1955.
There were an estimated 75,000 people crammed into
Stamford Bridge and it was so full kids were being
passed over people's heads so they could get to the
front. In the end they were let out on to the
greyhound track, although as it happens, I'd already
been there for ages because I wasn't going to bloody
well miss this game. This was the big one. This was
going to be the Championship decider. Getting to this
match was absolutely crucial, as was getting a
programme, because the first thing you worried
about was that they'd be sold out.

Anyway, what I especially remember was the
Billy Wright 'hand of God' incident – long before
Maradona came along. One of our amateur players,
Seamus O'Connell, hit this wonderful rising shot,
and from where I was, behind the goal, you could see
it was going in. Then suddenly Billy Wright leapt up
and punched it over the bar. But the referee gave a
corner. We couldn't believe it, but the linesman was

flagging away like mad and we were screaming at the ref to go and speak to him. Eventually he did and after what seemed like an eternity, he marched back and pointed at the spot. What a moment. Peter Sillett came up and cracked the ball past Bert Williams, right into the bottom left-hand corner of the goal. It was never more than six inches off the ground, and that was it. We were Champions with fifty-two points, the lowest ever recorded to win the League.

Only fifty-two points – yeah, but it was more than anyone else. But people still sneer at Chelsea. They still feel that somehow, perhaps because we picked up this reputation of being a bit of a poseurs' club or that we were effete, that if we ever did win anything it was because the tough, real men gave up. And there's still an element of that in the way that people write about us now, as if somehow we're never going to be taken seriously. Real men don't eat quiche, real men don't support Chelsea – it's all complete bollocks.

For me, the great Chelsea heroes will always be those I grew up with. I'm fortunate in that I'm personal friends with many of players now, which is great if you're a supporter. But there's nothing quite the same as having heroes. And the heroes for me are still people like the late Peter Sillett, Eric Parsons and Stan Willemse. But Roy Bentley is my all-time hero. I can't explain the thrill I feel when I sit next to

Roy Bentley, have a chat with him, put my arm round him and tell what it was like to watch him play. That's what being a football supporter is really about. Of course, that's not taking away anything from the likes of Harris, Bonetti, Cooke, Hudson, Osgood, Greaves – they're the sort of players who would make it into anyone's dream team.

But if all this was a high point for me, then the low point was, of course, the seventies. We were going nowhere. It was really miserable and the club was being run into the ground and the great team had been broken up. I'd always cheer Chelsea on, and I could always see something good in anyone that wore a blue jersey, but some of the players whose names I can hardly remember should never have played for Chelsea.

We went through a very barren patch until we nearly went bankrupt. Of course, it's great to have a great ground and see lovely football, that's the ideal combination, but in the end if they're playing magic stuff on the pitch, to be quite frank you don't care what you're standing in. But when you're standing in rubbish *and* watching it, that ain't funny.

The other depressing thing about Chelsea in the seventies were the number of racist thugs in the ground. I was on the GLC at the time, and I used to get in all sorts of scrapes remonstrating with those idiots. In fact, that's how I first got to know Ken Bates. I was so disgusted with what I was hearing that I wrote to Ken saying I'd been a Chelsea supporter all my life and I wasn't going to be forced out of the ground by these people. I asked him if I could come and talk to him about a few things. And Ken responded like he does and the club started to get rid of the racists. Whatever people say about Ken, he was in there, he arranged a meeting and we've been friends ever since.

Like everyone, I have to miss the occasional game due to work commitments. And because I'm so identified with Chelsea, it's no good me trying to make an excuse like I'm at a funeral or something on a night that we're playing at home. It's pointless. So I just come out and tell the Whips straight. Usually they will let me go. Let's hope it never comes down to a choice between a Labour government falling and Chelsea in a big cup game. It would be a hard one to call, but I suppose in the end it would have to be sustaining the Labour government! After all, Chelsea will go on forever.

There was one particular game against Sheffield Wednesday that I couldn't go to because I was speaking at the House, and that really annoyed me. I knew there was a vote coming up but a load of our MPs were down at the match, and the Whips asked me if there was any way of getting them back. So I phoned the club up and asked them to put out an announcement basically saying, 'To all MPs, there will be a vote at 9.30.' But it turned out to be wrong information. So the MPs came hurtling back to the House of Commons and there wasn't a vote. They weren't too happy. They thought I'd done it deliberately because they knew I couldn't go! Which of course wasn't true.

Chelsea are flying high at the moment and this success attracts supporters. But the true supporters are those who have stuck it out through the bad times. Football fans have had to change because the game is much more of a leisure industry now than it was. Sadly, this means some people are being forced out and this is a problem that clubs need to address. Football can decline in popularity just as quickly as it has risen. I can remember when it was in an awful state and attendances were plummeting. It is possible to envisage a time when football peaks and then starts to decline for a variety of reasons. What worries me is where the next generation of fans are going to come from. Because of TV, people pick up allegiances for clubs that play in cities in which they don't live and grounds into which they never go. So in the future, where are you going to get your loyal fan-base from? That's something clubs really do need to think about.

Chelsea is my first love but football is the game for me, and I am concerned about the future development of football. I'm left wondering whether in the next ten or twenty years people will be able to speak with the same enthusiasm about Chelsea, or

whatever club, as I can speak today. I had
opportunities to go to Stamford Bridge. It was cheap,
it was easy, it was working-class entertainment. I'm
still able to enjoy this, but I'm not selfish enough not
to be worried that kids may never be able to afford to
see the Bentleys and Silletts of today, other than on
the telly.

Eric Bristow

The thing about Chelsea supporters is that they seem to come from all over the place, not just one area but different parts of London, the Home Counties, everywhere really. I mean, I grew up in Stoke Newington, which is slap bang in the middle of Tottenham and Arsenal territory. In fact, my old house was walking distance from Highbury and my dad was a big Arsenal fan. That meant my first taste of football was watching Arsenal with the old man. In fact, the year they won the double [1971] the only game I missed all season was the Wembley final. But despite all that success, I was a Chelsea supporter at heart. I don't really know why, probably just to be different, but my dad didn't seem to care. He just liked me to go to football with him.

The thing about supporting Chelsea and living in North London was that Stamford Bridge was too far for me to go on my own. It was all right if you had a couple of mates who supported Chelsea to go with, but you weren't going to pop over there on your tod. Mind you, I suppose it's even harder for all those London kids who have decided to support Manchester United and teams like that. Serves them right really. I mean, you go to Hong Kong or places like that and they all support Man United. Why? Simply because they've seen them on telly.

So anyway, I was fed on a diet of Arsenal until I finally got to see Chelsea against Everton in the Charity Shield. Needless to say we lost 2–1, but at least I'd seen them. That's the team I remember, the FA Cup-winning side. I was only fourteen when they won those cups in the early seventies, but I can remember seeing the 1970 Final on telly, sitting there with fingers, legs and eyes crossed. Bonetti and Osgood were the players that stood out for me, and Charlie Cooke, who was a bit like the great Arsenal winger of the time, George Armstrong.

I never really played much football at school because I started playing darts when I was eleven, and that meant I didn't have much time to go and watch it either. All the boys have got their own teams on the darts circuit. Keith Dellor is a big Suffolk boy and supports Ipswich, while Peter Everson's a Chelsea boy. E-mails from the manager help me keep up with the news and the results while I'm away

One thing that's really puzzled me about Chelsea over the last couple of years was the Ruud Gullit business. I don't think we'll ever get to the bottom of that. They were doing so well. Vialli stepped in at the right time as far as he was concerned – I'm not being funny, but anyone could have taken over then and won the Cup Winners' Cup and the Coca-Cola Cup. I mean, the team was already there. I don't know Ken Bates, but he won't stand any nonsense and he sticks to his guns. I like people like that. He's upset a few along the way, but he says what he thinks. At least you know where you stand with him.

I go to Port Vale and Stoke sometimes because I get on well with Stanley Matthews, and now I live in the Potteries, I have to admit that I'm a Chelsea supporter that doesn't go to the matches. I watch them from my armchair, which is actually quite good for everyone else because when I do get a chance to go, they always lose. Which makes me a pretty bad omen.

Andy Cairns

I was four years of age when Chelsea and Leeds
played in the 1970 FA Cup Final. We'd left Belfast
and moved to a little town in Ireland called
Ballyclare, and I can remember all these mates of
Dad's coming round. I'd never seen anything like it
in the house before; I didn't know what was going
on. In fact I didn't even know what football was.
There were crates of beer everywhere. So I asked
my mum what was happening and she said it was,
'the football'.

The names of Chelsea and Leeds stuck in my
head as I sat and watched the game but I didn't
understand a thing, I just liked the colours and the
atmosphere. I vaguely remember the odd blasphemy
flying about. A lot of my dad's mates were Rangers
supporters, so they tended to side with Chelsea.
Names like Chopper stuck as well. It was like a
cartoon series, *Dastardly and Muttley*, or something

like that. I just thought it was a different world and it left an impression on me.

Northern Irish football, as you can imagine, was basically Glentoran and Linfield, while locally it didn't get much better than Ballyclare Comrades. Everybody tended to pick an English club, and where I came from most people picked Liverpool or Manchester because they had relations there. But I stuck with Chelsea.

When I was a bit older I got into Subbuteo and we got a little league going. The only other Chelsea supporter I knew was Ivor Owen and he'd managed to get over and see Chelsea – the lucky bastard's father worked for a domestic airline, so he got cheap tickets which made me extremely jealous. Ivor's a minister now believe it or not – from a seventies Chelsea supporter to a man of the cloth.

Then I discovered the guitar. I still kept an eye out for Chelsea and watched them on *Match of the Day*, but I didn't have the same passion as I do today.

It wasn't until 1992 that I finally saw a live game. It was a 0–0 draw with Everton. When I first got inside the Bridge I thought it was incredible and nothing like it looked on the television. I was standing in a corner of the ground by the East Stand which was basically just rubble. It looked like something out of Grange Hill, the kind of place where you get roughed up by tough lads called Baz and Spaz. I was really excited about it and there was a great atmosphere. It wasn't quite what I'd expected, but it was still brilliant. I kept looking at the football, then the crowd, then back to the game, trying to take everything in. And that was me hooked. Seeing the ground made so much difference.

We did a world tour during the mid-nineties and I didn't see any football at all for two years. We were in America a lot of the time and ended up in Arizona for the 1994 Cup Final against United. One of our technicians, who was a Liverpool fan, was going to phone his wife to get the result. He came back a couple of hours before we were due to go on but he didn't say anything. 'They lost, didn't they?' I asked. And he replied, 'You don't want to know'. 'Go on, tell me,' I said. 'How much was it?' 'Four–nil,' he said. I was gutted. I thought he was winding me up first, because that's the sort of thing that goes on all the time when you're on tour. So I phoned my father and all he could say was, 'You don't want to know.' It didn't put me off the gig, but it was one of those things that was on my mind before we went on stage. Afterwards was the bad bit, because a lot of our crew were Man U fans, as was our manager, who thankfully wasn't there, but he did manage to fax me at some ridiculous time in the morning, just to take the piss.

Because we've got so many supporters of different teams attached to the band there are a lot of arguments. But people tend to sulk rather than exchange blows. A friend of mine, Buzz, is a press officer, and a big United fan. He's obsessive about Man U and he detests Chelsea and literally won't touch anything to do with them. He came round one night and we'd completely decked the whole house out in Chelsea regalia and he was absolutely livid, he was furious. We were playing football on the Playstation and we had a small bet on the outcome and at the end of the night I owed him £20. Now I'd just been sent a Chelsea newsletter so I got the envelope, put the money inside it and handed it to him and he wouldn't touch it. So I left it on the table and he eventually got one of his mates to take the money out for him.

Pat Nevin and Charlie Cooke stand out as my favourite players. I remember Kerry Dixon as well, he had one of those names you remember. I saw him play in the FA Cup semi-final for Luton and he got a tremendous reception from the Chelsea lads. I still have nightmares about Craig Burley. Those backpasses were unforgivable. Even now when I see him playing for Celtic or Scotland my mates say to me, 'You still haven't forgiven him, have you,' and they're right. Coming back from Villa Park after losing the semi-final to United was dreadful. It's not his fault but it's one of those things that will always stick in my mind.

Usually a crowd of about ten of us meet up before the game in the pub and everyone's talking and chatting away, but you can tell they're just thinking about the game. I really get involved but I get so nervous. I've always been bad with nerves, before concerts and things like that. I was terrible on my wedding day. I suppose a football match is like my wedding and a gig all rolled into one – ninety minutes of sheer hell for my nerves. It's horrible. I have all these little things I do like crossing my fingers to bring luck, and there are certain clothes I won't wear to games if we've lost when I've been wearing them before.

Therapy? are a rock band and although it would be good fun to do a football song, we'd probably end up sounding like the Cockney Rejects or Sham 69, which wouldn't be very good for the club's reputation because people would link it all back to the seventies again. 'Blue is the Colour' is a fantastic song. There's something quite joyous and happy about it which is what I like. It's not a 'Knees Up Mother Brown' or anything like that. I might do it during a solo spot in the middle of a set one day, you never know.

Barbara Charone

Midweek Sports Special has a lot to answer for! Back in 1978 I was a music journalist and I came to England to write Keith Richards' authorized biography. I ended up holed up his house in West Wittering, all on my own, and *Midweek Sports Special* was one of the few things on the telly I looked forward to. I'd always played sport in America but never football. Sure, baseball is a good game if the weather's nice, and bits of American Football are exciting, but overall it's too stop-and-start, so they can get the adverts in. But football seemed to have it all. I loved it.

When I first came to England in 1974, I was just interested in football as a whole rather than just Chelsea. I'd seen them on the telly a couple of times but I didn't really start following them until I moved to London. I was living on Sloane Street, which is close to the ground. In fact, I can still remember hearing the police sirens going off when a game had finished!

People just presume that because I'm an American woman who's in the music business, that I know nothing about football – but how wrong they are. My office is a shrine to Chelsea and all my music memorabilia seems to have been pushed out, or to one side. Of all my football possessions pride of place goes to a limited-edition shirt signed by the European Cup Winners' Cup Final team. I'm also quite fond of a ridiculous blue hat – but I only wear that on special occasions.

Because of my job I get to meet pop stars all the time, so for me it's actually a lot more exciting when I meet footballers. Mind you, I met Tony Adams in a restaurant once and that wasn't particularly exciting! Dennis Wise, on the other hand, is wonderful. He's skilful, committed and great fun and I truly believe the only reason he gets sent off so much is because his reputation precedes him.

As for my greatest day supporting Chelsea, I can never quite make up my mind. I remember when the team ran out at Arsenal on the opening day of the 1984–85 season. The Clock End was absolutely packed. I couldn't believe we'd got there and that I was in on the start of a whole new era for the club. I got teary-eyed when the team ran out. Then of course there was the FA Cup Final against Middlesborough. WEA Records produce Suggs, and from the start both he and the club loved 'Blue Day'. We certainly had some laughs recording it. Some of the boys like Michael Duberry and Eddie Newton are really into their music, and Zola can play the piano, but not many of them can sing! So all in all it was a great day because as well as winning the Cup we had our record echoing round Wembley, and I had Roberto Di Matteo to score the first goal. But I suppose if I'm honest, that night in Stockholm takes some beating. Like so many other supporters, I remember those awful midweek nights at the Bridge when the stadium was empty, it was raining and Grimsby or someone like that were the visitors. It was terrible, which is why it's people like us that can really appreciate what's happening now.

It's no surprise that Manchester United figure strongly in my worst Chelsea days. First there was the 4–0 defeat in the 1994 Cup Final. That had started off as such a sunny day but ended up being one of the bleakest in every way. The other game which I hated was losing the semi-final to United at Villa Park two years later. Why on earth didn't Hoddle take Terry Phelan off? Everyone watching knew his hamstring had gone and it was obvious they were going to whip us down that side. Going back a bit further, I remember travelling up to Scunthorpe in the Milk Cup and we lost 4–1. We were down 3–1 after fifteen minutes. I think that's the closest I've come to giving it all up. We'd been relegated again

the previous season and had then failed to win any of
our first six games of the new season. But thankfully
I stuck with it, because of course we ran away with
the Second Division in the end.

I always used to prefer it when we were winning
every game in the old Second Division rather than
struggling for points in the First. That used to get
really depressing – going up one season, down the
next then up again. The Dixon-Speedie-Nevin
partnership was special. Pat was a great player and
he quite often used to pop into our offices in Soho. I
remember we used to shout 'Jesus and Mary Chain'
at him, because he was one of the only players who
liked indie music.

During my time supporting Chelsea we've
certainly had some duff strikers. I used to hate Alan
Mayes with a vengeance, and then this hatred passed
on to Mark Stein, and then Paul Furlong. It might
sound harsh but it's great to know they'll never wear
a Chelsea shirt again. I remember when John Hollins
resigned; it was my birthday. A friend pushed a note
under my door telling me he'd been sacked and I was
so happy because we were going nowhere under
him, although Campbell and Porterfield weren't
much better.

I try to fit my work schedule around Chelsea and
as Director of the Chelsea Pitch Owners I'm in
regular contact with the club. These really are great
times for Chelsea, especially when you look back and

see how things used to be. And it wasn't that long ago. It's impossible to overestimate Ken Bates' role in this success. He gets a lot of stick, but I think the fans know that Chelsea wouldn't be where they are today without him.

Roddy Doyle

I grew up in Dublin and if I tried I could probably count the number of times that I've been to see Chelsea. Like a lot of Irish people who follow English clubs, we have to do so from afar. Thinking back, I suppose there are two reasons why I started supporting them. I remember watching the 1967 FA Cup Final with my father. He used to watch everything on the telly but he'd rarely stray from his armchair, which was appalling but I suppose he was comfortable. He never actually got round to committing himself to one team or another either, so he didn't really influence my choice. Anyway, I decided I was up for Chelsea even though they lost that game, and it kind of stuck.

The other reason was because I was at an age where you had to choose a team. You were a freak if you didn't. At that time it was all Manchester United, Leeds or Liverpool. But I wanted to be a bit different and there was another friend of mine who supported Chelsea. This all coincided with the fact that if the wind was blowing in the right direction, we could just about pick up *The Big Match* in Ireland. There was always a London game on so I got to see Chelsea quite a lot. *Match of the Day* was a bit less predictable, both in terms of the games they showed and the standard of the reception.

Very quickly I realized that then, during the late sixties, Chelsea were a really great team. Charlie Cooke was my childhood hero and a lump still comes to my throat when I think about him. A friend sent me this great photograph of Cooke as a thank you present. It's here in front of me now and basically it will stay on my desk for the rest of my life.

Chelsea have got a tradition for having Scottish players but it's not so strong when it comes to the Irish. There was Paddy Mulligan in the early seventies, and of course John Dempsey, who wore big boots to protect his ankles. But that was about it, although at the time any Irish player playing in England was almost guaranteed an Irish cap because resources were so thin on the ground.

I was twenty when I finally managed to get to my first home game. It was a horrible occasion and we were beaten 3–1 by Leeds. It was 1978 and I was in London as a student but working as a road-sweeper for Westminster Council at the same time. Chelsea weren't a good team then. They were appalling. I stayed in London until the end of November that year and I had the opportunity to go to the Bridge every other week and it became like going to watch your own death.

The Leeds game was an ugly affair. There was a lot of tension, as there always was in those games, the football was bad and Tony Currie was the only real star of the show – and even he was starting to get fat. I left early in the end because there were fights breaking out all over the place and it all seemed so pointless. On a brighter note, the other game that really sticks out from that season was against Bolton which Chelsea won 4–3. That was a glorious, mad occasion.

I've managed to see Chelsea a few times when they've come over to Ireland on pre-season tours. They played here in Tolka Park once, I think it was against Shelbourne, and Gordon Durie, one of Chelsea's latest signings, was playing. That's also when I found out about this supposed link between Chelsea, Linfield and Rangers. There were a lot of supporters from both these other clubs at the game, all singing about King Billy and the Battle of the Boyne. I must admit, I'd never really associated Chelsea with sectarianism! Linfield and Rangers yes, but I can't see an Orange Parade going down the King's Road.

As well as Charlie Cooke, who as I say was my favourite player, I'm sure I won't be the first person

to list Pat Nevin as one of my all-time greats. I
thought the combination of him, Dixon and Speedie
was glorious, but they never really got the
recognition they deserved.

Of the current players I think Poyet is
extraordinary and I've a great fondness for Dennis
Wise. There seemed to be times when whether or not
we stayed in the First Division depended on Dennis's
availability. There was always a spell before
Christmas when we were losing everything and
Dennis would come back from injury or suspension
and suddenly the rot would stop. He was the only
class player we had for a long time and, again, he
never got the recognition he deserved.

I remember going to see them in the Fourth
Round of the FA Cup against Everton in 1992.
Beardsley was playing for them and Clive Allen was
in the Chelsea team. It wasn't a good side and I think
on paper Everton were probably better, but we beat
them. The atmosphere was fantastic and there was
that usual expectation that having won one game we
were going to have a great run in the cup that year.

There was a lot of genuine wit at that game, too.
A lot of the time all you get is idiots around you,
saying the same old crap time and time again. Mind
you, having said that, a lot of this particular stuff
was directed at Peter Beardsley, and it wasn't very
complimentary. But to his credit he was laughing
as well.

I remember Andy Townsend was playing for us, and Vinny Jones. I was always under the impression that Jones was brought to protect Townsend, but in fact it was the other way round and Townsend had to keep going over to Jones to tell him to calm down, and getting him out of tangles.

We're all atheists in our house and in the absence of religion I've introduced football. Unfortunately, my two boys didn't follow the script too well and have actually ended up supporting Liverpool. I brought the eldest over to see Chelsea against Liverpool a few years back, when we demolished them 4–1. It was a strange experience. On the one hand I was absolutely thrilled at the way Chelsea were playing, but on the other I had to contend with my son crying into my shirt, God love him! I would have done anything for the score to be reversed – just for a short while at least, until he stopped crying. At the very end of the game he was standing there in his Liverpool shirt, still sobbing away, and I was patting him on the shoulder telling him to remember the good things that had happened that day, like seeing his hero Robbie Fowler getting off the bus. Anyway, while all this is going on, this guy in front of us turns round, pats him on the shoulder and says, 'Poor little c**t!' But he said it from the heart, like one father to another! It was a great moment.

Andy Fletcher

I was born in Nottingham but moved down south when I was about two. My dad was a big Forest fan and from the age of six or seven he used to take me to Stamford Bridge with his uncles when Forest were playing. I actually learned my alphabet at Chelsea reading the letters round the ground into which they used to slot the half-time scores.

I've always considered myself hard-done-by because I was only a little boy during Chelsea's 'Golden Era'. Obviously I remember winning the FA Cup in 1970. We went berserk at school and I remember running round the playground with all the other Chelsea supporters. We all got a bit carried away and ended up hoisting the school hero, Bobby Tappin, (who actually went on to play for Chelsea in the Football Combination) onto our shoulders and then doing a few more victory laps as if we were the team.

Chelsea is our name

We lived out in Essex and it became quite an experience going to Chelsea. Most of the local people were West Ham fans, so when me and a couple of mates got the train into London we really had to run the gauntlet. It was quiet scary and every time we set off we used to hope West Ham were playing away. If they were playing at home we used to have to leg it past all the West Ham fans at Barking station and I remember getting my scarf nicked once – it was the fashionable thing to do in 1974. I don't know what they did with it; burned it I suppose.

I started going regularly when I was fourteen or fifteen, but the club were on a downward spiral by then. There were a lot of dreary games, but I do remember one particular FA Cup match against Sheffield Wednesday. We were 2–0 down with about fifteen minutes to go and I'd gone with a friend who supported Wednesday and he couldn't believe his luck. Then incredibly Mickey Droy scored twice and Chris Garland added another and we won 3–2. But there weren't many days like that.

Of course, you couldn't avoid the violence in those days. I remember once, for some reason there were about 3,000 Tottenham supporters on the left-hand side of the Shed – I was in the middle. Suddenly the Tottenham fans moved toward us to try and 'take' the Shed, and the next thing I knew I was being carried fifty yards to the right and then a hundred yards the other way by this mass of bodies as the Chelsea fans pushed back. It was quite exciting, but scary as hell too.

One of my saddest Chelsea moments involves Pat Nevin. He was trying to be a pundit on some music magazine around the time when Depeche Mode were starting out and he gave our single a real slagging off. We were mortified because he'd been a hero, and his words probably hurt us more than anyone else's. I've met him a couple of times since but I have to be careful because the rest of the band wanted to punch him.

Dave Gahan (lead singer of Depeche Mode) was a real Shed boot-boy when he was fifteen or sixteen. I didn't know him at that time, but he stopped being a Chelsea fan when he became a New Romantic. It didn't really fit in with the image of a Chelsea fan then, though it might do today!

I carried on going to Chelsea when I was in the band. I'd started sitting on the benches and I had to walk past the Shed to get to my seat. People used to shout at me – not because I was famous, but because they thought I was Howard Jones! It was really embarrassing because I was abused for being the wrong person.

When Depeche Mode really got going in the eighties, I could only go to occasional games, but in the last ten years I've been going regularly and even travelling abroad to see them play. When Chelsea played Viktoria Zizkov in the Cup Winners' Cup last season I travelled out to the Czech Republic on the same plane as the team. On the way back we were just about to get on the plane when I saw all these policemen running towards me. Of course, having a naturally guilty conscience, I started wondering what on earth I had done. But instead of pulling out guns, they had autograph books in their hands. The players didn't know who I was and just stood there, wondering why the police were getting my autograph and not theirs.

We ended up in Vancouver on our recent US tour and one of our riggers, who is a massive Chelsea fan, tracked down this pub on the Internet where the local branch of the Chelsea Supporters' Club meet. So he turned up one evening and it just happened to be their monthly meeting, with about sixty ex-pats there. They all came along to the gig and then the next day I was inducted into the Vancouver Supporters' Club. It was such a big deal; it was serious stuff, I had to do a speech and everything. But it's interesting to see how many supporters there are around the world – they're the biggest supporters' club in Vancouver. The same's true of Mauritius. I've been there a few times and there are millions of Indian Chelsea fans there, which just goes to show what a global game it is now.

When I'm in America I always make the effort to track down a telly if a Chelsea game's on the box. For the 1998 FA Cup Final I was in LA and we had our after-tour party the evening before the game. I didn't roll in until 4 a.m. and I had to set the alarm for 6.30 in the morning so I could get to this bar to see the game. I ended up running for an hour to get there on time because there were no taxis at that unearthly hour. Of course, it was worth it. The place was full of Chelsea fans and then Di Matteo scored after forty-two seconds. Even my wife made it for the second half.

I actually played at Stamford Bridge last year in Kevin Hitchcock's testimonial against Spurs. Suggsy was playing too. It's such a hard game to play and the players deserve all the support they can get. Pat Nevin is still one of my favourite players, even though he slagged us off, because he was so exciting, and that's one of the reasons I was so upset. I liked the battlers too. David Speedie was good, he had real commitment and I've liked Poyet since he joined the club. David Lee was always a favourite and it's a shame that he never made it, because he's the sort of guy who never really did anything wrong.

There's quite a lot of the music crowd who follow Chelsea and some of us, like Suggsy and Dave Baddiel, go for lunch quite often. It's a very close-knit circuit and we make a real day of it. The only disappointment for me is that my wife has started coming along. It used to be my only way of getting away from her!

Derek Fowlds

For me, it all began when I was thirteen and I used to visit my nan, who lived in a big house on Clapham Common. I was living in Berkhampstead at the time and I would meet up with my cousin Bernard, who was six years older than me, and he'd take me to Stamford Bridge. I didn't know much about football then, other than the fact that I enjoyed having the odd kick-around at school. But if anybody ever asked me which team I supported, I'd always say Chelsea, without any hesitation.

My first introduction to Chelsea, and football in general, was seeing Roy Bentley charging around as centre forward in a ground which was packed but completely open to the elements. Those early days of going with Bernard have really stayed with me. I never, ever followed another team, whereas today I find a lot of youngsters support the team that are always winning. Sad really, isn't it, although I

suppose they're all coming to Chelsea now. But the
real fans are those die-hards who have watched them
through thick or thin, through the tragedy and the
farce, and who have suffered all those jokes. Chelsea
were so inconsistent for so many years, it was
incredibly frustrating.

For most of the sixties I had to support Chelsea
from afar, but I finally got a season ticket in 1970
after we'd won the FA Cup. I kept that seat, CC93 in
the East Stand, until five years ago but by then I was
away so often filming *Heartbeat* in Yorkshire, that it
wasn't worth keeping it. But when I can I still go
with Clive (Mantle) and other friends. And when I
finish *Heartbeat* for good, and I'm back in London,
I will be a season ticket holder again.

In many ways acting has always got in the way of
supporting Chelsea, but I can't complain because I've
had a great career. People often ask whether
presenting *Basil Brush*, which I did for five years,
stopped me getting to the Bridge, but when it first
started, *Basil Brush* was on a Friday. Not that that
pleased everybody. I remember someone arranged a
petition at Euston Station which was signed by about
300 businessmen complaining that they couldn't get
home in time to watch the show, and would we please
start showing it on a Saturday. Always happy to
oblige, we started recording the show on a Thursday
and from then on it was tea-time fare after the
football results. I must admit, I haven't seen Basil for

years. He was a Spurs supporter by the way. There's a lot of Arsenal and Spurs fans in showbiz too, but I suppose you can't win them all.

After that, in 1979, I was in *No Sex Please We're British* for a year. By then I was taking my youngest son Jeremy to the matches. My eldest son was never interested. Anyway, dear old Jeremy was five at the time and he still tells his mates he had to wait until he was eighteen before he saw Chelsea win a game. I used to lift him over the turnstiles in those days, and sneak him in, which I shouldn't be saying really, because Ken Bates will want his money back.

Anyway, curtain up was at 5 o'clock, which meant I could still go to the Bridge with Jeremy but I had leave at half-time. Jeremy stayed with my friend Basil – the human rather than the vulpine variety – and he took him home for me. That season obviously wasn't one of our best, because I used to phone Basil later that night and ask him what I'd missed and he'd always say, 'Oh, nothing, Derek. Nothing at all.'

You do have to be careful supporting a club like Chelsea, because you can become so engrossed in what's going on that the slightest set-back can have such a dramatic effect on you. I remember we were playing Liverpool in the Cup a few years ago and I rather pessimistically presumed we were going to get thrashed. I was in another play at the time and because of a matinée performance, I couldn't get to the game. I decided I didn't want to find out the result until later that night, because I was convinced we'd lost, and knowing the score would have put me in a bad mood for the evening performance. But someone let it slip that we'd won 1–0. I couldn't believe it and I went on stage that night and, my God, what a performance I gave!

When you sit in the same place year in, year out, you look forward to seeing all the boys and chatting and catching up on news. For me, going to Chelsea has always been about a lot more than just watching a football match. You hear about births, deaths, marriages; it becomes a very social happening. We just loved going to the Bridge, and I suppose that means we also loved suffering. We suffered for so many years. If we won a game it was like winning the pools. But we had great fun and they were good days, even though we struggled in the League and got knocked out of the Cup in the third round every year. We stayed because we loved Chelsea and we loved going to Stamford Bridge. That's what we did on a Saturday.

That said, I do remember things did once come to a head, when we very nearly went down to the Third Division. Passions run high when they lose and you get frustrated, so myself and my friends had a meeting and simply asked ourselves, 'What are we doing watching this crap?' And we decided that we didn't actually come for the football, it was to see each other. Thankfully things have since improved

rather dramatically on the pitch and now we're a
class act. But it's been a long time coming.

My high point of supporting Chelsea has to be
winning the FA Cup in 1970, with that wonderful
team we had then. And until three years ago, we had
to keep going back to those years and that team,
because we hadn't won anything else. I see Ossie now
and again and Clive and I just go down on our knees.
We bow in front of him! He's such a normal guy, as
they all were, but the entertainment they gave us
was phenomenal. And Charlie Cooke. Oh, what a
player. Of course, later we had another Charlie
Cooke in dear old Pat Nevin. There's been some odd
players too over the years, I can tell you. All those
years in the wilderness. But we'll gloss over that.

Another highlight for myself and Clive was when
Joe Irmani, one of the club's directors, invited us
into the directors' box. We met Ossie there and he
was doing his usual matchday stuff and he asked us
if we would come and draw the raffle during half-
time, out on the pitch. So we went down to the
tunnel, and I said to Clive, 'Do you realize what
we're doing? We are actually coming out of the
tunnel on to the hallowed turf. Now let's do this in
slow motion because we're not going to do this again
– ever.' So they announced Clive Mantle from
Casualty and Derek Fowlds from *Heartbeat* – God,
we didn't half get some stick. And I looked up to
where I used to sit and they were all acting like

Roman Emperors with their thumbs pointed to the ground, baying for blood!

I met a few of the directors that day, and every time I've met Ken Bates I've enjoyed it. He's a tough businessman who's achieved great things, and I'm sure Matthew Harding would have done the same. The first time I met Matthew, who I knew was a great fan of *Basil Brush*, was in the Imperial Arms pub before a game. He came up to me straight, right out of the blue, and sang the whole of 'Basil the Farmer, the Knight in Shining Armour' to me – it was a very emotional moment! Then to round it off we sang the *Basil Brush* song together.

Bates has done a tremendous job for Chelsea and I only wish the two of them could have worked together, because I think they both loved the game and the club. Which is exactly how I feel. I love Chelsea and they've given me years of endless pleasure. I still get a great buzz when they run out onto the field, and my only wish is that Ossie was still playing. Up the Blues!

Andy Hamilton

My brother took me to my first game when I was five.
It was against Newcastle in 1960 and we won 4–2.
Ron Tindall was the centre forward at the time and
he scored a hat-trick, and I always remember they
were all headers. After that I went sporadically until
I was about eight, and then I started going every
week.

This was before the old West Stand had even
been built. In those days that part of the ground was
one huge terrace that just seemed to go on and on for
ever. It was immense and really high. If you think
the back of the Shed was a long way from the pitch
you should have tried standing in the old West
Stand. But I loved it. When it was full – and in those
days you could get crowds of over 50,000 inside
Stamford Bridge – the atmosphere was unbelievable.
The only seating then was the old East Stand, or the
'Chicken Run' as it was called, and the tumbly-down

North Stand, which always looked like it was going to fall down at any moment. Behind that, of course, were the greyhound kennels, and then the cemetery.

I grew up next to the cemetery, in Ifield Road, about five minutes' walk from the ground. When I was very little I remember hearing the crowd on matchdays and I always knew when Chelsea had scored.

Of course, when I first started to go to matches with my brother, I was only one small kid in a huge crowd of people, but I got used to it. I was very trusting and you knew that the blokes around you would make sure you didn't get trampled on. Sometimes you still got squished and crushed but if it got too much, they tended to pass you over their heads down on to the greyhound track. I had to get to the ground very early to claim one of those stanchions to sit on, because I wouldn't have stood a chance of seeing the game otherwise. Later on, in a fit of fraternal love, my brother made be a stool in woodwork at school and I used to take that with me. It was a bit more practical than trying to find a stanchion, because you could take it to away games too. You probably wouldn't be allowed in the ground with it these days.

My brother was a big fan but my dad wasn't really that interested. He did become a supporter in later life, but that was more of a social thing. I went to school not far from the ground and most of the kids were Chelsea fans. When I went to secondary school there were a fair number of us but also quite a few Tottenham fans, because they were the Manchester United of the day. They were the fashionable club for kids to support when I was a child, in the wake of them winning the double in 1961.

I went religiously every week all through my school years and it only stopped when I went to university. I did a fair bit of travelling to away games, either in the car with my brother or on Inter City football specials. It was a big thing to travel to away games then and I remember getting back to Euston late at night on countless occasions. As the violence increased the specials became a pain, because they'd get held up all the time. You certainly weren't a valued customer on one of them. They were a laborious experience. We played Leicester on Boxing Day once and it took us bloody ages to get back because all the Shed Boys got pissed up and kept pulling the emergency cord. Then we got thrown off the train and we had to get a normal train.

I suppose the ultimate away trip was the 1970 Cup Final replay at Old Trafford. I'd already been to Wembley for the first match and then I bunked off school for the second one. I was fifteen and I had to get my mum to fake a letter saying I wasn't well, which, of course, nobody believed.

Chelsea got relegated during my first year at Cambridge University, but as soon as I got back to

London in the mid-seventies I got a season ticket in the East Stand. There were some good times then but the club was pretty much in the doldrums, especially under Geoff Hurst. Then things improved a bit under John Neal, when the likes of Nevin and Dixon were in the team and they got a bit more attack-minded.

I saw some pretty depressing games and when I think about it now, they all blur into one huge 0–0 draw with Oldham or someone like that. There was a time when the team didn't seem to have a single creative player in it. I remember when players like Tony McAndrew were around and you just thought there wasn't a player in the side who could pass the ball. But I did like that team that Neal put together, particularly Pat Nevin. I loved watching him because he was such a throw-back. He was very skilful; he was different. I enjoyed watching Speedie to begin with until he got so paranoid. He didn't start out like that – he began as a player who was very focused and then somehow he got this persecution complex. He just thought the world was against him. Then he started getting in fights and I got very irritated by him in the end. I liked Dixon in a way too. I admired him. I thought he was an honest player and on his day he could finish. It seems bizarre now that once we used to have to look to players like Colin Lee or John Bumstead for inspiration, when we've got players that can play in every position. It's a laugh when you think we had players who couldn't even control the ball, but we did.

My dad was a fan of Doug Rougvie. He was popular but he was more of a comedy sideshow than a great player. He was so clumsy and his judgement was suspect to say the least. I always wonder how he managed to get into Aberdeen's first team, let alone win any Scotland caps. But he was a character.

I was never very enamoured with Vinny Jones, not only because he couldn't actually play but also because his hardman image was a bit overdone. He was so slow that he couldn't actually shut someone out of the game and it wasn't as if he was such a great tackler that he could dominate their midfield either. I thought his reputation was a bit inflated really and it meant that Townsend had to do ten times the work.

I think people who grew up on the terraces have got a comic view of football. At Chelsea you used to stand there in the cold and rain and very often it was only the company that you went for. It certainly wasn't the football. That is what has made Chelsea supporters better equipped at coping with adversity. I've always thought that the last ten minutes of a Chelsea game were distinctive because we always seem to be hanging on. You'd start off a game thinking 'We're doing well here' and then we'd always end up with that anxious last ten minutes, a habit they still haven't completely got rid of.

There's a lot of individual humour in the grounds which you absorb, and I'm sure a few examples have popped up in some of the scripts I've written. One thing which I've always thought was incredibly eccentric, and incredibly Chelsea, was the first time I heard the 'Celery Song' at Plough Lane, where the crowd were very close to the pitch. They started singing the song and at the end of the chorus they lobbed all this celery into the goalmouth and the goalie cowered instinctively, presumably because he'd sensed stuff coming at him. But he ended up looking very silly as sticks of celery and other vegetables landed around him. I loved all that sort of thing. I remember during the early sixties the crowd used to sing 'Strolling' by Flanagan and Allen and I miss that. It was a great sound, as good as West Ham singing 'I'm Forever Blowing Bubbles'.

I never thought about giving it up but I had kids and started playing regularly again, and that changed my attitude to weekends. I've drifted away from going, primarily because I don't want to wipe out the whole weekend. Sadly Robbie, my son, is an Arsenal fan. I don't know why he did it. It's just something that happened. But I can handle it. I've come to terms with it. It's not a problem – honest.

Paul Hardcastle

To be honest with you, there are two things that
really make me anxious – watching Chelsea and
flying. I get totally wound up doing both – they really
get my heart going. If I watch a game on the telly and
I don't have a good few beers during the match, then
I'm in a terrible state at the end of it. I heard
someone died in the Shed once and I'm not surprised.
Watching Chelsea and flying just don't do me
any good.

I've been Chelsea all my life. I was born in St
Mary's Abbots, which is just a couple of miles down
the road from the Bridge. The first time I can really
remember supporting them was against Spurs in the
1967 Cup Final. I was living in Germany at the time,
because my dad was a musician too and we used to
move around quite a bit. I remember seeing it on the
TV and Tottenham were 1–0 up and like the little
shit I was, I started shouting 'Go on Tottenham'

simply because they were winning. Anyway, my mum turned round and said, 'You can't support Tottenham, you were born in Chelsea' and that's how it all started.

Back in England, I went to school on Edgware Road and it just so happens I was in the same class as Phil Daniels, another bona fide Chelsea fan. Obviously we went our separate ways after school but I bumped into him at the Bridge last season. Gary Crowley, the DJ, was another Chelsea supporter who used to go to our school, as did Tony Grealish, the old Northern Ireland player. One night I particularly remember was when we beat Leeds in the FA Cup Final replay. We were living in Victoria at the time and again I watched it on telly and I can remember people going past our house all night screaming 'Chelsea'. That was cool.

My first Chelsea game was away to Arsenal in 1970 when we won 3–0, with over 50,000 packed into Highbury. I remember seeing us lose 5–2 to Leeds too. I think we played them six times that season, including the FA Cup Final. That particular day the Leeds fans took over the Shed. I was standing there and I couldn't believe what was going on around me. I'd gone with a couple of mates but I didn't know where they'd disappeared to, so I had to climb up a floodlight pylon. It was a bit heavy. I was only about two foot tall at the time, but I was up that pylon like a rat up a drainpipe. It was a very frightening experience, but it didn't really put me off. To be honest with you I just thought the violence was a bit of a laugh, simply because I didn't really understand what was going on. I used to just get out of the way.

Of course, it all started going wrong when the Cup-winning team broke up. In terms of players, everyone always remembers Osgood, Cooke and Hudson, but it was Alan Birchenall who really stood out for me. He was brilliant. I thought he was a stunning player. And I also used to like Ian Hutchinson too, with that huge throw of his. He may have only played about 150 games for Chelsea but he was one of those players who seemed to be around forever. After that there wasn't much in the way of entertainment for years. David Speedie was a great little player but he wanted to beat everyone up, and Kerry Dixon was a great striker but he was a bit lazy, wasn't he? But then saying that, he scored a lot of goals for us, so he must have been doing, something right.

I suppose I drifted away from Chelsea and when I started taking a real interest again the team seemed to made up of a bunch of dwarfs with the arrival of people like Mark Stein, Dennis Wise and John Spencer – all really small guys. Where had all the Droys, Wicks and Bill Garners gone? Even Gavin Peacock was short. But we'll let him off, because he was such a thorn in Manchester United's side. He always used to score against them. The only big bloke

we had then was Paul Furlong and I don't know if he
got a fair crack of the whip. Everyone used to have a
go at Stein too but when he first joined he was the
most prolific scorer in the Premiership. It's funny but
quite often strikers who used to score goals for fun,
like Casiraghi for example, come to Chelsea and just
dry up. The worst example of that is Robert Fleck –
he used score every minute for Norwich and then he
come down here and he was crap.

People remember the mid-seventies as the worst
episode in Chelsea's history, but it was pretty bleak
during the Ian Porterfield years too. I mean what he
did to Beasant was unforgivable. That guy was a
good goalie but he made a couple of blunders, which
everyone does, and Porterfield says 'You'll never play
for Chelsea again.' It was disgusting. But now he's
forty and he was the one who stopped us winning
about 5–0 against Forest the other year.

Of the current team, Zola is a special guy and
probably my all-time favourite. I think some people
went over the top with the Laudrup thing. I think
you should take your hat off to him. He could have
just stayed for the money, but he didn't. He obviously
wasn't up for it, so he left. I get asked to tour a lot
and I could make a lot of money, but there are times
when I just don't want to do it.

For years, the most embarrassing thing about
Chelsea was that we were always getting knocked
out of cups at an early stage by teams from the lower

leagues. Most of my neighbours are Tottenham and Arsenal supporters, so every time we got knocked out by some sodding little team, I got stick. Thankfully they can't say much nowadays, after the 6–1 and 5–0 wins. Mind you, I still had mates after the Arsenal game saying they had their reserve team out, but I pointed out that their reserve team cost £19 million, while ours was just £13 million! They made nine changes, and we made eight. We just had a better side. And anyway, we knocked them out of the same cup the year before.

As well as surviving away trips to the likes of Wigan and Crewe, the other thing that has really changed is that we don't give away goals in the last few minutes anymore. In fact, we're more likely to score these days. I remember the 2–2 game with United a couple of seasons back. My ex-manager is a big Manchester United fan and he got some great tickets. We drove to the ground, walked straight into the lift, and there were drinks waiting for us when we arrived. And the view was absolutely stunning. The funny thing was, a friend of mine, who was also a Red, was sitting there all frustrated because we were winning 2–1, but surprise surprise, we did it again that day and gifted them a late goal.

I sometimes sing at games, but I must admit I find it hard picking up the words sometimes; 'One Man Went to Mow' – what's that all about? Where did that come from? Obviously a lot of people

remember me for the song '19' and strangely last
year we lost 19 games and this year we went 19
games unbeaten.

Last year I met Dan Petrescu on holiday. We got
talking and he asked me to send him some CDs of my
music, and then I got a call from him out of the blue
inviting me to a game. I had a superb day out and I
decided then that I wanted to get more involved with
the club. So I got in touch and now I'm doing some
music for the TV channel.

I scored a goal in front of Dan on that holiday. In
Sardinia there's a place where all the footballers go
called the Forte Village, and it's got all these special
natural pools which are meant to help players get
over pulls and strains. Zola had been there a couple
of weeks beforehand, and while we were there Van
der Saar was booked in, as was Moriero who was
there showing off and walking round with bouncers
on either side. But that's one of the things I liked
about Dan, he was so down-to-earth.

My only gripe with Chelsea is that we don't
always start playing for half an hour. I sometimes
wish I was always late because I feel so nervy during
that opening period. We seem to play Coventry at the
start of every season and let two goals in during that
first third of the game. There's always that little
lapse in concentration. So please Chelsea, change
just one thing – start *playing* at three o'clock and
save my poor jaded nerves!

Mark Hillsdon

There used to be a perversity about supporting Chelsea that I've never really understood. When they first got under my skin we had a ramshackle ground, bar one state-of-the-art stand that had nearly bankrupted us; men in charge who were more interested in their next free lunch than the next fixture; racists on the terraces; and a team bereft of skill, class and style. Supporting Chelsea was a challenge, a holy grail, which only a chosen few could attempt to undertake – at least that's what I told my schoolfriends who were Tottenham to a man, while my Dad swore allegiance to Arsenal. Perhaps I did it just to be different, or perhaps out of some misguided loyalty to my elder brother, a man brought up on the heady success of the early seventies, and who to this day still denies a brief flirtation with Spurs in the mid-sixties.

My brother's bedroom was a Mecca when it came

to Chelsea memorabilia. This was a time when the great stars were beginning to fade – but hidden within a huge pile of his old *Shoot!* magazines, Peter Osgood, Charlie Cooke and Peter Bonetti were still fresh-faced twenty-somethings. Once, when builders inadvertently brought the ceiling of my brother's room crashing down, the whole exalted contents of the room ended up in the back garden. Among the books, records and ancient football boots, I found an old colour copy of the *Evening News* celebrating Chelsea's cup wins of 1970 and 1971 and felt a sudden kinship with the shepherd who discovered the Dead Sea scrolls.

As I lived in North London, Stamford Bridge was a bridge too far for most of the seventies, and I had to content myself by playing out my fantasies on the Subbuteo pitch. Thank God for Subbuteo, because whatever Chelsea may have lacked in the real world they more than made up for on the green felt, with an unprecedented haul of silverware. Doubles were won with monotonous regularity, trebles were common and even quadruples weren't unheard of as the Blues swept all before them. More often than not it was Spurs that felt the full force of the blue plastic in various finals, as an attack featuring the likes of Tommy Langley, Clive Walker and, for a brief period Lee Frost, sent Tottenham reeling. Not surprisingly this success at domestic level was translated into European glory too, as teams like St Etienne, made up of players named after words gleaned from elementary French lessons, such as Pupitre, Stylo and Fenêtre, succumbed to Mickey Droy and the boys.

During this time it was hardly surprising that Chelsea players made little impact on the England team. Even Ray Wilkins only managed twenty-four caps while at the Bridge, and the nearest we really got to a regular was physio Norman Medhurst sitting on the bench. But in the world of Subbuteo, John Bumstead, the Garys – Chivers and Locke – and Kenny Swain were regulars, while even the ex-pat Steve 'Jock' Finnieston had three lions painted on his chest when Tommy Langley was in the treatment room with the Evo Stick.

My first taste of live football was at Highbury to see the Liam Brady-inspired Gooners beat Norwich. My second was at Stamford Bridge, in the East Stand, on 2 January 1978. West Brom were the visitors. I was taken by George, a wealthy friend of my Dad's, and was accompanied by his son and grandson. We drove across North London in a Jensen, one of the smoothest cars on the road at the time, but as my stomach churned in the back seat, I longed for the suspension of my dad's Cortina. Bill Garner scored twice that day and the scrawled signature of Ian Hutchinson across the front of programme is testament that I must have met the great man, but sadly my only true recollection of the day is the equally stomach-churning trip home.

It was to be a couple more years before I went regularly. I came of age during the 1981–82 season, when I witnessed at first hand a Chelsea forward line of Colin Lee, Alan Mayes and Phil Driver on far too many occasions. A Friday night game in Leicester sticks out. I was met outside the school gates by my brother, his girlfriend and fat mate Spence, all squashed into his Triumph Dolomite. We motored up the M1 to witness a 1–1 draw, with Borota in typically eccentric form and Mike Fillery, always a favourite, scoring for Chelsea. The game also featured my first introduction to those classic tunes, 'Get out your riot shields' and 'You'll get a boot wrapped round your head', before a freezing journey home – the heater had broken – with only a Beatles compilation for company. Happy days.

In fact, we made it to a few away games that season. We witnessed a Mayes goal at Orient; saw Micky Droy skidding around on the astroturf during the traditional Boxing Day victory at Loftus Road; managed to miss the first two goals in a 4–3 thriller at Charlton and even made it to Paul Canoville's début at Crystal Palace. Sadly the main reason I remember that was the fact that a large minority of Chelsea supporters dragged the club's name through the mire again with their chant of 'get him off' for the game's final twenty minutes. Canoville was the first black player to play for Chelsea.

As usual, expectations were high for the start of

1982–83 season, and with the Dolomite still going we
made it to Cambridge for the first game of the
season. Crammed into to one tiny corner of the Abbey
Stadium, one die-hard supporter made it up a
floodlight pylon, anti-vandal paint and all, despite
the fact that he was on crutches. Pop Robson scored
the winner in the sunshine as Chelsea embarked on
their most disastrous season ever. (Even Tottenham
managed to stop an unprecedented quintuple at
Subbuteo when a late Mark Falco goal snatched the
reinstated Watney Cup from Chelsea's grasp.) Of the
thirteen games I saw that season, five were 0–0
draws and we failed to score in two of the others.
Even a few pre-match pints of Dog Bolter at the
Ferret and Firkin failed to raise our spirits. That was
also the season my brother and I began to invent
games to keep ourselves entertained during matches.
We'd crack feeble jokes about making a mess with
our nuts as we gobbled some of Percy Dalton's finest,
and once even hallucinated that the hot dog trolley
making its way into the visiting supporters' enclosure
in the North Stand was in a fact Trojan horse,
concealing Chelsea's hardcore who were out for a
rumble. It really did get that bad.

So it was with some trepidation that I put all my
hopes into a blond-haired striker called Kerry at the
start of John Neal's third full season in charge. On
Sunday 28 August at least one butter manufacturer
was happy as the words 'Kerry Gold' appeared atop a

Chelsea report for the first time. Five-nil against Derby. The next game I saw he scored all four against Gillingham and then two more in the 5–3 rout of Fulham. Clive Walker's late winner at Bolton the previous April seemed a long way away.

Gradually the visits became more sporadic and were limited to midweek games – my brother was by now married with a kid. That said, the 1984–85 season did take us closer to Wembley than we'd been in over a decade as we stormed the Milk Cup with those epic replays against Sheffield Wednesday (where were the Canoville baiters then?) before the tragedy of the semi-finals against Sunderland.

Then I moved to Manchester and it seemed that everyone I met was affiliated to a team that humiliated Chelsea during the 1986–87 season. A Forest fan revelled in the 6–2 thrashing, West Ham supporters laughed at me after the 5–3 débâcle at Upton Park and even my best mate, for God's sake, supported Wimbledon. I didn't know whether to laugh or cry after they beat us 4–0. Later I risked life and limb to cheer Roger Freestone's penalty saves at Old Trafford but was among friends when we beat Manchester City 3–2 in that Maine Road classic, when Tony Dorigo scored in our promotion season. I abused my power as editor of Manchester Poly's magazine to print a picture of Graham Roberts on the front cover to celebrate our Zenith Data Cup victory in 1990, and four years later I found myself in an executive box at Old Trafford and nearly caused a riot when Gavin Peacock scored. A few weeks later I stood in a state of bewilderment as Robert Fleck scored in the last match in front of City's famous Kippax. In fact, that state of bewilderment persists today. The Cup Final defeat followed a few weeks later, but apart from the occasional blip, we haven't looked back since. Who could have imagined that a club which once consecutively employed Ken Shellito, Danny Blanchflower and Geoff Hurst as manager, would one day add the trio of Hoddle, Gullit and Vialli to the list?

Perhaps there's still a perversity about supporting Chelsea. I still find it hard to reconcile the success of recent years with those early games in the eighties. Personally I liked Stamford Bridge as it was – the club shop housed in a portacabin by the Bovril gate, the crap facilities (I even wrote a letter to Ken Bates once, berating the state of the toilets), the awful view from the Shed, the corners of the ground that hadn't been used for years. But most of all I loved the thrill of actually winning a game. Not just the shock cup victories over Liverpool, but those hard-fought battles against Watford, Wrexham or Shrewsbury Town. You'd leave the ground believing that we'd turned a corner, and that thought kept you going for at least another seven days, until some other mighty club paid a visit to the Bridge.

Clive Mantle

I'm proud to say that I'm still part of one of Chelsea's crews, although I hardly think we are figure too heavily in any police files. We call ourselves the BBC Chelsea Drama Mafia because, as the name suggests, the drama department at the BBC is completely run by Chelsea supporters. Our pre-match rituals in the pub before the game are sacrosanct and we get each other completely worked up with predictions about things that could go wrong. It's a very well-balanced crew, with a good cross-section of optimists and pessimists. And long may it continue. We take defeat very badly although we're a bit too old to go on the rampage.

Watching football is a huge pleasure for me, but it's not a relaxing pastime. I get so so tense and worked up that I certainly fall into the pessimistic camp. It's only when the final whistle goes that I feel relief. I was standing at Highbury last year in that classic game when we were 5–0 up, but I was still thinking we could lose this right until the end. I suppose that comes of supporting a club like Chelsea, with its infuriating reputation for inconsistency.

My allegiance to Chelsea has taken three phases. There was the childhood infatuation, then putting up with those stagnant years in the seventies and eighties and now the new era of hope.

I was about six or seven when I first became attracted to the club. I was first aware of supporting them in 1963 and it was really to do with the colour of the shirts as much as anything. That and the way the name looked on the page: 'Chelsea', it just seemed to stand out.

I was brought up in Barnet, North London, but I was spared from being a Gooner or following Tottenham or anything unthinkable like that. I saw the true path. I was only in school in London until I was ten and then we moved to Cambridgeshire. This meant I only got to see Chelsea during school holidays. One of my brothers was a Wolves fan – I've no idea why – and he always used to look out for the Wolves v Chelsea game at Stamford Bridge. So a 2–2 draw with Wolves in 1968 became my first game. It was pouring with rain and we stood by the dugout. You know, I can still remember, it was a really grey day but the colours on the pitch were just amazing. The blue of Chelsea and the gold of Wolves. It was such a spectacle. And that shirt worn by the likes of

Barry Bridges, with CFC in flowery writing, is an all-time classic.

The Cup Final in 1967 left me distraught. I can remember watching it at boarding school and the room naturally divided up between Tottenham and Chelsea supporters for the afternoon. Mind you, I resented all these temporary Chelsea fans who followed Leeds or Manchester United for the rest of the week, but were now suddenly supporting my team for the afternoon. But I made the best of it and held court with facts and figures about all the players.

My all-time hero is Peter Bonetti. I still remember my first pair of green cotton Peter Bonetti goalkeeping gloves. He was the first ever keeper to market anything and they were absolutely useless, but as a young goalkeeper I thought, 'Well, I've got the gloves, now I'll be able to catch anything.' But on a wet day they just got soggy after a minute and that was it.

Nowadays there's an embarrassment of riches when it comes to great players, but I really do like Frank Leboeuf. Not only is he a great player but he's also a great character. I think Dennis Wise is a wonderful footballer but he infuriates me sometimes. Then again, if you did take that edge out of his game, would he be the same player?

Of the bad ones, Graham Wilkins does stick out I'm afraid. But when his brother Ray was at the club you never wanted to say anything too vitriolic about Graham in case Ray heard and decided he didn't want to play for Chelsea any more!

This, of course, was all during that terrible period in the seventies. When I think of it now, it all seems to have been played in black and white. I can't remember any colour except the odd moment such as winning 4–3 against Bolton. I was a student then and I used to get the tube to the ground but, in an effort to save money, I used to walk back. My flat was in Islington and I used to take a different route through London every week. Those walks had quite a profound effect on me. Chelsea had probably lost at home to some God-forsaken team and I was left thinking that it was my lot in life. It was probably raining and everybody else was going out on the town. I think that's why I took things more personally than just remembering a dodgy Gary Locke backpass or Tommy Langley missing a sitter.

Of course, I never considered jacking it in, even during the years of violence. I just made a conscious decision not to take anyone to the game with me, although of course the standard of football in those days meant people were hardly queuing up to come. I couldn't put people through it. I was prepared to endure it because it was in my blood and it became a kind of masochistic torture week in, week out. You'd make friends with the two or three people standing around you in the Shed, even if there was someone wazzing down your leg. I've never understood people who can swap a football team; people who say, 'Oh, I used to support Chelsea.'

I remember we had a team of very willing battlers in the seventies. I can't knock Fillery, Locke, Britton, those type of people, because they did try their hearts out, but they just weren't the full ticket. With Mickey Droy at least every time he went up for a corner something happened. Either he scored, or he pushed someone into a post and then landed on top of them. Those were highlights in those days.

I was there when we got relegated at Tottenham and Ray Wilkins was captain for the first time; when we nearly went down to the Third Division; and when Middlesborough beat us in the play-offs. But, in a perverse sense, that's when they needed us most. Personally, I think it was vital to live through those moments to fully appreciate being able to stand in the Rosunda Stadium in Stockholm and watch us win the Cup Winners' Cup or be at Wembley in 1997. That was the carnival Cup Final. Fifty minutes they were on the pitch afterwards, the longest ever. We wouldn't leave the stadium and they wouldn't leave the pitch. That said, all our subsequent celebrations have been getting shorter and shorter as we have been getting more and more blasé about winning things.

I've still got all my programmes and some scrapbooks covering 1966–1972. But pride of place among these possessions goes to a map I drew when I'd broken my arm. I was about fourteen and to relieve the boredom, I drew a map of Chelsea Island with landmarks like Cooke Bay, Bonetti Goldmine, Sexton Point, all that sort of thing. I sent it off to Chelsea and didn't think anymore of it until about a month later it came back and everyone had signed it. I'd missed out Tommy Baldwin and he just signed it in the sea somewhere! But what really delighted me was that there were drawing pin marks in the corners, so it had obviously been pinned up on a noticeboard somewhere at the training ground. I was really thrilled.

Acting does get in the way of the football – but not too often. It's terrible actually because I know at the beginning of next season I'll be on tour in *One Flew Over the Cuckoo's Nest*. I was offered another tour as well, but that would have meant being in the theatre for the whole of the football season and I just couldn't face doing that. The most annoying thing is doing matinées on a Saturday afternoon, which no one ever comes to see. I always arrange for one of the actors to come on stage with the score written on his hand for me. There's many ways of keeping up with important things like that while you're performing for a dozen people who are all asleep.

Over the years I have found myself justifying why I support Chelsea so many times and I've been indoctrinating my nephews and nieces since the year dot. I took them to the Full Members' Cup Final and I honestly remember wondering whether it would be the only time I'd get to take them to a cup final.

I'm very non-political when it comes to Chelsea. It's so easy to get peeled off into one camp or another and get sidetracked into the minutiae of should we be doing this or that. Of course, all those things are relevant and if there was something drastically wrong then I'd take a stand about it. But my principle passion is the football on the pitch. I'm the sort of bloke that if there is a rumpus going on in the stands, I'll still be looking at the football in case I miss something. That's why I go to the match. That and the camaraderie of the BBC Chelsea Drama Mafia.

David Mellor

I was always football mad as a kid, but growing up in a little town in Dorset, there wasn't that much access to top quality, live football. And it wasn't on the telly in those days either, so there wasn't the same pressure for people to pick and support a particular team as there is now. That didn't really happen until I came to London in 1970, after I'd been to university, and I found myself living an Ian Hutchinson throw-in from Stamford Bridge. So for the first time in my life I had top quality football on my doorstep, and I soon became very keen on the club.

I remember standing in the Shed for my first game against Spurs. I was a bit naive in those days. It was a horrible afternoon and pouring with rain so I thought I'd better take my umbrella, but I was soon told where to put it once the proceedings began. I was wearing what I thought was a decent overcoat too but it obviously wasn't as well made as I had been led to believe because the collar, under the provocation of this water, turned up like a dry sandwich and I could never get it back again.

Unfortunately, in those days the Shed was just a vast bowl of humanity. Some people get very sentimental about the terraces but I have to say that while there was an animal excitement about it, it was a bloody uncomfortable way of watching football. Personally, I like being able to watch the game without being worried whether the next human wave is going to wash me away. But gradually, as I got a bit more money in my pocket, I used to buy tickets for the West Stand.

I have to say that as the seventies wore on, the gilt wore off the gingerbread of Chelsea. Some of the great creators were either prematurely transferred, like Peter Osgood, or retired. The standard of football went down and the standard of crowd behaviour went down even further. I became increasingly troubled by this, whether it was the activities of extreme right-wing groups or people who were just yobs.

A point came when I felt I could take it no longer. I hated the racist abuse and without being old womanish about it, I almost felt violated hearing some of this stuff. I think it was fairly prevalent in English football as a whole but there's no doubt that Chelsea had a particularly bad problem. I think there were a lot of organizations out to exploit the name of

Chelsea, and the culminating point for me came in another game against Spurs. For some reason Chelsea fans always get too worked up about this fixture. A couple of Tottenham supporters were sitting in front of me and one of them was cheering. Then all of a sudden this fellow behind me leaned across, and using my shoulder as a pivot for his left arm, he smacked the Spurs fan round the face.

Enough was enough, so for a season or two I went down to Fulham. I was the MP for the adjoining consistency of Putney at the time and a conscious effort was made to woo me over to Fulham by Ernie Clay, the then chairman. I once had quite a high opinion of him, but as it later turned out he was one of the worst type of football club chairmen because he was only in it for what he could get out. And in the end he sold Fulham down the river.

Fulham were in the old Second Division then, as indeed were Chelsea, and I soon came to appreciate that you can't support a club where the board has no ambition. I got very disillusioned very quickly. Then, at a match between Chelsea and Fulham, I had a very happy encounter with the new owner of Chelsea, Ken Bates. He bounced over to me – and I didn't know him from Adam – and said, 'You're Chelsea really aren't you. You're not really a Fulham fan.' He was right, of course, but I said that, without wishing to sound pompous, I didn't feel that a Member of Parliament should be caught up in the kind of bundles that developed last time I went to a Chelsea game. He simply replied, 'I don't have any time for all that stuff. We've got a real battle to secure the future of the club and I would like your help.'

The club had been driven into the ground and nearly bankrupted by the new East Stand. Ken had bought the club and its debt, but he hadn't bought the freehold of the ground, and he anticipated a hell of a lot of trouble over its future. I've always taken the view that the ground is not an optional extra for a football club, it is the club. There was lots of talk about building a new stadium on the edge of the M25, but this was all being spouted by people who were going to make a lot of money by getting rid of the ground, and selling the land for houses. So in effect what he said to me was, 'Let's have a meeting, discuss things and hopefully you can come back.' And I've been back ever since.

I took the view that as a football fan I was entitled to a have my say about the future of my club, and I had quite a lot of impassioned encounters with people over the future of the ground at enquiries and meetings about planning permission, which I attended on the club's behalf. One of the reasons why Ken and I get on so well is that I was always there ready to help him, even when people wouldn't give you tuppence for Ken Bates, or for Chelsea Football Club and its future. And he recognizes this. People were laughing in his face when he said Chelsea were going be one of the great clubs in Europe. But now look at us.

I have to say that while throughout my whole life I've been a Chelsea supporter, it's only over the last fifteen years that it's become a real passion. Naturally, I brought my kids up to be Chelsea fans. I remember the headmaster of my youngest son's school giving a lecture to parents about why they should take their kids to the opera, and that they could be relied upon to discover football and discotheques for themselves. But to my mind that was a rather simplistic view. Football gives kids a sense of loyalty and belonging.

One of the reasons I'm so up for it at the moment is that I think there's more to come. I actually think that there's a critical mass of talent at Chelsea, and if it can be organized properly, there is no reason why we shouldn't go on winning. And now you can say that and not have everyone around you fall about in hysterics. You've got to believe that Chelsea can't go back to where we were – that's my passionate belief.

I've had some great times with Chelsea and some bad times. I've seen them relegated more than once, I've seen them floundering in the Second Division and I can remember old Graham Roberts falling into the mud during that humiliating defeat by Bristol City in the FA Cup. He just couldn't stand up. But by far the greatest moment was going out to Stockholm and watching them win the Cup Winners' Cup, because Ken has always wanted to lay to rest the ghost of the seventies team and not have people keep saying that was Chelsea's glory time.

I was in New York on holiday when we played that third round tie against Manchester United last January. We spent most of the time trying to find out where the live broadcast was, because we knew an Irish television company was screening it, but every bar we went to denied knowledge of this. Then, bizarrely, we were at our New Year's Eve dinner and a waiter came up and says, 'You're David Mellor aren't you? I'm a great football fan too.' And he told us to go to O'Flanagans on 81st Street, and the match was on at 10 a.m. the next day. It was on a time lapse and I had to ring a friend of mine on a business matter and I asked him not to tell me the result. But at the end of our conversation he told me to get ready for a 'very interesting game'. So I thought to myself, 'This doesn't bode very well.' But we went to this bar in any case, and I can tell you, it's the first time I've ever drunk five pints of beer before lunchtime. As every goal went in I got more and more depressed.

I've always led a fairly stressful life and for me the great joy of football is that I can go down to Stamford Bridge and forget about everything else that's going on. It's a wonderful escape. If I can fit business in around the fixture list then I do, and a number of people who thought they were going to have a quiet evening have been dragged along to a football game with me.

I always feel much more up for *606* when I've been to a live game. The adrenalin's still pumping. There's nothing worse than sitting in a studio, which I have to do when Chelsea are away. We've had some total disasters in the past when I used to watch Chelsea away games too and we'd try and do the show from one of the BBC's studios outside London. I got so much abuse from the press about the expletives that came out when the lines went down, that we stick to London now.

As for the players, Peter Osgood was everything that was good about Chelsea. He was one of the King's Road boys. I always had a soft spot for Kerry Dixon too. But I do think that if anyone epitomises the new Chelsea, it's Gianfranco Zola. He's thirty-two, fit as flea and as smiley and pleasant off the pitch as he is on it. I soon discovered in politics that the bloke you saw on the telly wasn't the same as the person I used to see in the corridor. The mask slipped. But when you talk to Zola he is such a genuine human being. Another favourite is Gus Poyet. Now when old Gus had his knee problem he used to sit in the row behind me and I remember one occasion when, having limped in, he was out of his seat shouting his head off when Chelsea scored. He was up quicker than any fan. And I thought to myself that guy couldn't be more passionate about the club had he born at the gates of Stamford Bridge.

There's no doubt about it that there were long years of underachievement and all that changed with the arrival of Hoddle. I don't think Hoddle was ever the ideal Chelsea manager – you have to remember we finished eleventh the year he came and eleventh the year he left – but it did come together more towards the end.

I rub my eyes from time to time and think to myself that if ten years ago I had dared to say 'We are going to have a couple of people playing in the England v Italy World Cup qualifier, and by the way they're both going to be playing for Italy,' people would have thought I was stark raving bonkers. The transformation of the club has been incredible over the last fifteen years.

When you actually look at the club in the late seventies, not only was it in a terrible state in and around the ground, but it was terrible on the pitch as well. What Chelsea has done is build towards the vision of becoming one of the major clubs in Europe, as Chelsea should be. Even during the dark days, I remember old Bates used to say that Chelsea are only a mile from Harrods. He always believed that Chelsea had a destiny, because it was one of the only football clubs located in an attractive part of a big city. Though nobody's perfect, we all owe a huge debt of gratitude to Ken Bates for what he's done.

One of the reasons why I think he resented Matthew Harding so much was that he thought Matthew wasn't there when the real trouble was. And that's one of the reasons why he and I get on. We exchange our views very frankly with each other but he knows I was always there for him at the club when I was needed. The kind of people I like to meet in life are not chancers like Ernie Clay, who tell you one thing and do something else, but a bloke who gets on and tries to create his vision.

Brian Moore

It was during my last full year in rugby that I first
started going to Chelsea. I'd been sent off for treading
on someone, accidentally of course, but I still got
banned for nine weeks. I was living in Parsons Green
and with some spare time on my hands, I decided to
go down to watch Chelsea. I really had no idea I
would enjoy it so much.

I suppose people could accuse me of being a
Johnny-come-lately supporter, but in my own
defence, I played rugby every Saturday for eighteen
years and never had the chance to watch any other
sport. I thought about watching rugby but decided
against it because I didn't want to become one of
those sad ex-players who wander up and down the
touchline with people coming up to them saying, 'You
should still be out there playing.' I just wanted to get
cleanly away from the game. I didn't want to get
sucked into that world.

I grew up during the time when Osgood and co. were playing and I've kept an eye on Chelsea ever since. They're a glamorous team and one that has always played good football. I got a season ticket last year in the East Stand middle tier but I've moved to the Matthew Harding Stand now. The East middle was full of people talking bollocks about tactics and slagging off the players – as if they could do any better. Having listened to some of the comments around me, I've decided that when you've got a background in sport you develop a different way of looking at a sporting event. I think you can see things tactically which other people can't because I was quite astonished at the stuff some of the people were coming out with. It got frustrating because I could hear all this noise coming from the Matthew Harding Stand and the Shed, yet I was stuck in the East middle.

When I actually sat down and watched a game at Chelsea, I was completely taken aback by how much I enjoyed it. The difference between watching live and watching on the television is so vast. You see so much more; you see things more tactically; you can see people who are working and those that aren't, who would be off-camera on the TV.

I take clients and friends to games but it has always been a rule of mine that I would only take a client if I thought they would enjoy it, and I thought they were sports-minded. I'm really not into corporate entertaining for people who have no interest in the game and just sit there making nonsensical comments. The other criterion is that I would only ever take clients that I got on with, because you've got to sit next to them for an hour and a half.

I get very sucked into a game and am quite amazed when I find myself in mid-rant. I have to remind myself that I'm a solicitor and I really should know better. My language has deteriorated appallingly since I've been going, but then again it's no worse than anyone around me.

I used to marvel at the way Mark Hughes played. He was my type of player and very professional. He could look after himself, too. Normally it's the defenders that bully the strikers, but watching Hughes play it was the other way round. He was superb at giving a dig here and a dig there – just letting the defenders know he was around so they didn't take liberties. But along with that was his ability to run at people and his tremendous ball-skills, astute flicks and through balls. He had a tremendous repertoire. Even watching him at the end of his career, when his legs weren't what they were and some of the speed had gone, you still had to marvel at the way he approached the game.

Mark Hughes would definitely have made it at rugby and I think Wisey would have made it as a scrum-half. If he played rugby he would have soon learned that you can't do certain things. Firstly, referees can march you back ten yards if you give them any gip, and secondly, if you gob off at an opponent you get whacked, simple as that. And there are enough big people out there to do it to you. It's not like soccer. In rugby there's always a time when someone is not looking and you'll get it if you carry on. But because Wisey's got brilliant footballing skills and he's tenacious, he would have adapted. The game would have knocked that lippy edge out of him. Of course we would have had to look after him. But in rugby, if his ill-discipline continued and it cost us points and games, then it would be us that would have sorted him out without a second thought. And that did used to happen if a player stepped out of line. They tend to shut up and get on with it then because they know these people are quite capable of making their point.

There's a massive difference between supporters of rugby and soccer. They're far more vociferous at soccer, but I think the level of understanding of the game is higher in rugby because more of the crowd has played the game. Soccer fans are prepared to cheer the team when they're trying but not playing particularly well, whereas rugby fans just tend to go quiet.

I'd much rather have played in a football atmosphere every week. Of course, when internationals came round we had crowds twice the size of an average Stamford Bridge crowd. And they were fantastic. But with club games week in, week out, we'd never get anything near approaching it. It wasn't quite a man and his dog but it wasn't packed either. It must be fantastic to play in front of huge crowds at Stamford Bridge every week. That's why I can't understand why people sometimes play in such a lacklustre way. With all that noise and expectation, the adrenalin should be pumping round your body. It shouldn't just be about money. But because I was never a professional perhaps I'm just a little too sentimental about it.

I have some contact with the club but not much. I knew Matthew Harding and my company did the conveyancing for Di Matteo's restaurant but that's about it really. From one sport to another, although there is a natural affinity between players, people are often very reticent and won't necessarily just go up and shake each other by the hand, like actors or people like that. There's a natural reservation; it's almost a sense of embarrassment really. You don't like to intrude.

I met Ossie, Chopper Harris and other players at a reunion dinner a few years back. I remember I sat next to Peter Bonetti, with Chopper on the other side next to Tony Banks. Everyone was asked to stand up and say a few words and when it was Chopper's turn he just launched into Tony Banks, saying what a boring git he was and advising everyone to vote

Conservative next time. He really gave it what for, which wasn't quite in keeping with what you expected to happen!

I sometimes get recognized at games. I remember we were playing Sheffield Wednesday, and I was nipping away quickly and this bloke shouted out something along the lines of 'Why don't you go back up north you fucking northern bastard.' I stopped dead in my tracks and started to stare at him. He went as white as a sheet and spluttered out, 'Oh, not you Brian! I meant him on the pitch.' But the look on his face was an absolute picture – it was all I could do not to laugh.

John Motson

I shall never forget Christmas Day 1957. My late
father, who at the time was the Superintendent
Minister of the East End Methodist Mission in
Commercial Road, Stepney, produced a present
neither of us were expecting. A fellow clergyman of
his, the Rev. Jimmy Butterworth – famous for his
youth work at a centre called 'Clubland' in Central
London, had invited us to Stamford Bridge as his
guests, to watch Chelsea play Portsmouth.

You need quite a long memory to recall the time
football was regularly played on Christmas Day. The
matches were invariably in the morning, but while
the spectators then went home for Christmas lunch,
the players spent the rest of the day travelling,
because more often than not, the two teams met in
the reverse fixture on Boxing Day!

Back to 1957, and our seats were high up in the
old North Stand – the one that used to be curiously

perched in the corner, just to the right of the main stand and to the left of the open terrace. We had heard about a seventeen-year-old prodigy called Jimmy Greaves, who had scored over 100 goals in reserve and youth team football the season before, and who had marked his first division début with a goal at Tottenham on the opening day of the 1957–58 season.

With his long white shorts and stealthy running action, the young Greaves bore all the hallmarks of a fifties hero – not one of your actual teddy boys exactly, indeed his gait was almost sheepish – but a war baby brought up in that tough hinterland on the borders of East London and Essex.

Born to be a star he certainly was, although his father, who was a tube train driver, had long conversations with other clubs before he and young Jimmy agreed to sign for Chelsea.

A lot of Jimmy's friends went the same way – including another young man from the Dagenham area called Terry Venables. Years later, Terry used to recall travelling across London in Jimmy's car, and stopping at a café for roast beef and Yorkshire pudding (Jimmy's dish, not Terry's) before they played in a home game!

But Terry had not reached full professional age when Jimmy made his bow in the first team. Greaves' colleagues in Chelsea blue that Christmas morning were Reg Matthews, Peter Sillett, Wally

Bellett, Len Casey, John Mortimore, Derek
Saunders, Peter Brabrook, John McNichol, Ron
Tindall and the England amateur international
Jim Lewis.

All I can remember about the game is that
Greaves scored four stunning individual goals, the
type we were to see so often in the years ahead for
Spurs and for England. Maybe time has coloured the
memory, but I seem to recall also that the late Peter
Sillett, who had a fulminating right foot, scored from
somewhere near the halfway line.

What is certain is that Chelsea ran out winners
by seven goals to four, and a twelve-year-old
Methodist minister's son went back to boarding
school after Christmas to tell his friends about the
fantastic match he had seen at Stamford Bridge.

Oh yes, and what was I saying about the way
they used to play the return matches? The following
day, Chelsea lost 3–0 to Portsmouth at Fratton Park!

Pat Nevin

Being brought up in Glasgow, I was always a Celtic supporter as a kid, but of course I had to be a bit different, so when my dad asked me what I wanted for Christmas one year, I think it was around 1969, I naturally asked for a Chelsea strip. It was the first strip I ever had and I chose it because it was stylish, just like the team. That's what I liked about them, but needless to say I was the only kid in our street, if not the whole of Glasgow, to have one. Nobody else had even given Chelsea a second thought because round where I grew up it was Celtic or Rangers, and that was it. I must admit my interest dropped off when they were in the Second Division but during the period of Ossie and Charlie Cooke they were my favourite English team.

I'd actually turned Chelsea down a few times before I finally signed in 1983. I'd told them I didn't want to be a football player, I wanted to study and finish my degree. I finally decided to try it out for a couple of years and took a sabbatical from my course, which I still haven't finished to this day. I've got a year to do and I know full well I'll never do it.

It was Ian McNeill, John Neal's assistant, who spotted me. Clyde were asking for £85,000 and it went to a tribunal in the end. I can remember Ken Bates looking at my height and my weight and just saying, 'No'. It was left to Ian to convince him. In the end Bates said to him, 'OK, but your job's on the line with this one,' and Ian very, very bravely agreed to it. I only had to talk to John Neal for ten minutes to know he was someone I could work with, and I've still got a lot of respect for him.

London suited me because I was a city boy anyway. I was young and independent and felt comfortable and relaxed about what I was doing. I think I annoyed the club by insisting I lived my own life and rent my own flat but I couldn't face going to live in digs. I refused to have any of that.

Two or three seasons into my time at Stamford Bridge I remember I actually tried to tackle someone in a game and of course I came off worse. I went over on my ankle which meant I missed the last match of the season against Liverpool. Naturally I still wanted to see the game, but rather than sit with the other players I decided it would be a perfectly sensible to stand and watch the game from the Shed. The other players thought I was mad.

I suppose I was quite popular at the time so I went along thinking to myself that I'd have a chat with a few people and it could be quite a laugh. I was there for ninety minutes and not one person even said hello! I could hear a lot of people saying, 'Is that him? He's scruffy enough. No it can't be.' But in the end they ignored me for the whole game. It was quite eerie really because had I been out on the pitch they probably would have been singing my name. It was great to be in amongst it. It was a splendid thing to do, it really was, because you get a great feel for things and in fact a year or two later a couple of other players copied the idea.

To be honest, it was always difficult for me to tell what my relationship was like with Chelsea supporters, but I think they latched on to the fact that I was doing things out on the pitch for my own enjoyment, whether they worked or not. Obviously that was quite an unusual attitude to the game and they were quite taken by that. But they knew I worked hard as well.

I used to walk to games when I lived in Earls Court and chat to supporters on the way, and when I moved to Pimlico I used to get the number 11 bus down the King's Road. But that all had to stop quite suddenly one day. I hadn't realized the subtleties, if that's the right word, of the situation between Tottenham and Chelsea supporters, and the fact they didn't like each other. At the time my two flat-mates were Tottenham fans so I used to go along to watch their midweek games, standing on the Shelf. Can you imagine it now – Pat Nevin standing on the Shelf! But Chelsea were in the Second Division then so it was dead easy and Spurs had some great players like Hoddle, Hazard and Ardiles, who I wanted to see.

The next season Chelsea went up and by then I'd cottoned on that there was a bit of antagonism between the fans, but I hadn't realized how deep it went. Anyway after one match between us I decided it would be quicker if I got the tube home rather than a bus. So I was standing there minding my own business when this big Spurs fan came up to me, and I realized immediately I'd made a very, very big mistake. The guy pulled a knife on me and said, 'Your name's Nevin, innit.' So I said in my best 'mockney' accent, 'Nah. What you talking about mate?' He was a real bonehead and just stood there staring. Everyone else on the tube had suddenly produced an *Evening Standard* and were intently reading the classifieds, so I was left wondering how on earth I was going to get out of this one. Then of course the tube stopped in a tunnel. So he said, 'Who's your favourite player then?' which showed you the IQ of the guy because as if I wouldn't know the name of a Spurs' player if I'd just played against them. So I said, 'Mickey Hazard' and that shut him up until we finally got to the station. But as I went to get off he blocked my way, so I shouted in my broadest Scottish accent, 'What the fuck's that up there?' I couldn't believe it but he actually turned to have a look, so I thumped him one and legged it. He started running down the platform after me but two policemen suddenly appeared, so he had to get back on and the last he saw of me was my grinning face. I got a taxi home the rest of the way and by the following Tuesday I'd bought myself a car.

I left Chelsea for Everton in 1988 and my first trip back to Stamford Bridge was a strange experience. I came on as sub and scored, and that's the only goal I've ever scored and not celebrated. We got beat 2–1 in the end but I couldn't bring myself to celebrate a goal against Chelsea.

Now I'm back in Scotland I get very few chances to go and see them. But just after I'd finished playing for Everton, and moved to Tranmere, Chelsea were visiting Goodison Park. I wanted to see the game but obviously I had a problem – whose supporters do I go with? I was always going to go in with the fans rather than with the boring, middle-class corporate lot. I wanted to go in the working-class end, as it were. It wasn't a hard decision to make and I just went in with the Chelsea boys. But I thought to myself that it was only two or three months since I'd been playing for Everton, so I'd better keep a low profile – big long coat, collar up and all the rest of it. I was confident that even though I'd played for Chelsea for four or five years they weren't going to say anything. So I took my seats with a couple of mates and after about ten minutes the whole end started pointing at me and singing, 'There's only one Pat Nevin'. It was like being spotted at a party which you're not meant to be at – really embarrassing, only 30,000 times worse. Everyone was looking to see if it was me and these pissed off Everton supporters were saying things like, 'The wee shite, he's only ten minutes away from here and he's bloody supporting the opposition.' But I didn't and still don't have any negative feelings towards Everton. I just knew I was going to offend somebody.

Chelsea have gone far, far beyond anything we ever hoped to achieve when I was playing. And that's great for the fans because they deserve it. They used to travel everywhere with us and out-sing the opposition every time. I remember once playing Wigan and I decided to go back up to Scotland after the game. So I just jumped on the train and of course all the Chelsea fans were on it. We had to change at Crewe, but before that me and my dad had a brilliant time just chatting to the Chelsea supporters. I always felt very comfortable in their company.

Paul Oakenfold

It all started, as I'm sure it did with a lot of people, when my mum and dad bought me a Chelsea shirt some time in the seventies. Nothing strange in that, you may say, other than they both supported Arsenal. My dad used to take me and my brother down to Highbury quite a few times but I just didn't like it, something just wasn't right, so I kept on pestering him to take me to Chelsea and he finally gave in.

My first game was Stoke City in about 1976 and that was it for me. I was living in Kent at the time and the local teams were Dartford, Gravesend and Gillingham – so of course, all the kids supported London teams. When I moved to Streatham, where the big team was Crystal Palace, the fact that I supported Chelsea took on a whole new significance. That's when I started getting stick and having fights at school. There were probably three of us who were Chelsea fans and we played Palace in the FA Cup and it was murder. That was one of the times when I got beat up, but I stuck to my guns and I've always been Chelsea. And always will.

I was really into football at school and I had trials with Tooting and Mitcham, but they wanted me to train twice a week and play on Saturdays, and by then I'd found music, clubs and girls, so I was out of there! I hung my boots up. I did play for the English DJ XI against the Italian DJs in Rimini a couple of years ago. We beat them 4–1, but although mentally I was still up to it, I ain't got the legs anymore. I hadn't realized how slow I'd got.

We used to stand on the left-hand side of the Shed. Of course, I wanted to go in the middle where all the lads were, but I couldn't see from there. What's really stuck with me is the vastness of the whole place and that little tin stand in the far corner which used to have a band playing in it. Weird stuff.

I gradually started going away too and I had to start lying to my parents. I was going on coach trips that they didn't know anything about. I think Hereford was my first away game – what a start! I went up to Leeds as well and the bus got smashed up – they bricked us basically. Somehow my parents found out and they banned me from going to away games for a bit after that.

But I soon started again. I remember going to Molineux at the end of the 1976–77 season which was great because that's when we went up. There

weren't meant to be any Chelsea supporters there
but we were! We were real die-hards. I met up with
this firm of lads and we used to go every week.

But there was a lot of violence too. Coming back
from Newcastle once on the train they got in amongst
us and run us all over the place. That's when it was
all going off. I wasn't involved with it, I just had this
unerring knack of always being in the wrong place at
the wrong time. At Bristol City, for instance, I ended
up in the wrong end. I got absolutely battered and it
was a really frightening experience. Even at home I
got in the way when West Ham took the Shed, that
was terrible. They came in and all of a sudden people
were running everywhere. I also got crushed outside
Crystal Palace. They weren't great times. It certainly
wasn't a case of saying, 'Yeah, it was fucking great,
we did this and we did that.' It wasn't good at all.

But what really put me off for a bit was when the
club were going through a really hard time. I'd saved
my pocket money up, as you do, and I remember on
the way to the ground there were these big bins
which you used to put your coins in to help 'Save the
Bridge' or something like that. I was doing all that
and then the club whacked the prices up. So I
thought to myself, 'I'm doing everything I can as a
young supporter and I'm getting nothing back in
return.' So I stopped going for a bit because of that
and the fact that it was just becoming too violent. For
the money that we were giving the club, the return

was dreadful. And the team was fucking hopeless at
the time, too.

One of the few good moments at the Bridge
during that time was playing the New York Cosmos
and it was great to see Beckenbauer and all those
kind of players. As for Chelsea, Ray Wilkins was one
of the first players I really remember. After that
Clive Walker was a favourite, and then nothing until
Dixon and Nevin arrived.

One of the strangest things that has happened to
me as regards Chelsea was when I found out that my
cousin had married Mickey Droy. I couldn't believe it.
It was a right touch. I ended up getting his shirt from
when he broke his arm. I stitched it back up and used
to play round my way in it and no one used to believe
that it was his. I don't know why I wasn't invited to
the wedding. I wasn't DJing at the time, not that
they'd have liked the music I play anyway.

Things have changed a lot at Stamford Bridge.
I'm still a big singer at the games but where I sit now
it's all the execs, so it's boring as fuck. There are four
of us who are pure hard-core sitting among these
corporate twats in shirts and ties and we're all
shouting and hollering and they're all looking at us.
They've tried to move the loyal supporters out so they
can use it as a corporate section and fill it with twats.
But I won't budge. If I wasn't successful now, I
wouldn't be able to afford it. The normal supporters
who have followed Chelsea through all the hard

times, how can they afford to take their two kids to
see them nowadays?

Of course I take supporting Chelsea seriously, but
I try not to let it affect my moods to the point where
it's going to ruin my day. I've got friends who really
get the hump when we lose. But at the end of the day
you can't take it too far. The players certainly don't.
I've been in the players' lounge after a game and
they're all there having a drink and laughing. And
that's quite surprising because they've been out there
playing a shit game and now they're in the bar
having a drink. It doesn't seen right. Sometimes we
take it more seriously than the players.

There's definitely been times when I've certainly
sat there and questioned why I'm spending all this
money to see this team, like when we got knocked out
of the Milk Cup by Sunderland and there was all that
fighting on the pitch. That was a real low point. But
you always end up coming back.

Good or bad I've been there for the last twenty
years, and until recently we'd won fuck all, but
what's great about Chelsea supporters is that we
have a craic. I went to Everton when we lost 6-0 and
we were still singing. And I just stood there and I
was so proud to be Chelsea. Six nil down and we're
still singing louder than them. Chelsea supporters
can take the piss out of themselves as well as other
teams. Other supporters just get the hump. At
Manchester United, if they have a bad game, their

supporters just sit there giving them a hard time. And I'm like stood there saying, 'What are you like?'

One of my favourite wind-ups was on one of my best mates who's a Tottenham fan. I'm always telling him that I hope they never go down because we're guaranteed six points if they stay up. And when we beat them 6-1 at White Hart Lane I kept ringing him up on his mobile every time we scored.

Going to Stockholm was great. We went on a chartered flight that left at eight in the morning. Drinking all day, went to the match then straight back to the airport. It was like Dunkirk trying to get 10,000 Chelsea supporters back to England. I was delayed five hours and when I finally got home I could hardly stand up I was so tired. But they're the sort of things you do.

People I work with know I'm serious about Chelsea. My DJing is all booked around the fixtures list. If we're playing Aston Villa on the Saturday then I'll play Birmingham on the Friday night. I have to be within a fifty-mile radius of a match otherwise I don't play. The promoters now know this, so they check the fixtures and book me around that.

'Blue is the Colour' is a classic song, it's *the* football song, and it shouldn't be touched, but I would do a Chelsea tune if it was right. A few years back I was asked if I'd do the Tottenham record and I said, 'No way'. There was no way in a million years I was going to do that!

Peter Osgood

To be honest with you, I wasn't a Chelsea supporter when I was a youngster. I used to live in Windsor and follow the Arsenal. But then my uncle, Bob Snashnall, started taking me to Stamford Bridge. We stood on the big bank where the West Stand used to be. It was a massive terrace. Then we started to go to a few away games and the more I went to see them, the more interested in them I became. Of course this was the time of Drake's Ducklings, when all the young lads were coming through. Terry Venables was captain, Peter Bonetti was in goal, there were the Harris Brothers, and Jimmy Greaves briefly, followed by the likes of Bobby Tambling, Bert Murray and Barry Bridges. It was Uncle Bob who wrote to the club and got me my first trial with Chelsea, so the 'wits' in the dressing room used to call me the 'Man From Uncle'. It was storybook stuff really because within six months I'd gone from watching them from

the terraces to cleaning their boots. That might
not sound very glamorous now but for me it
was amazing.

As a supporter, no particular games stand out,
but I do remember watching Stanley Matthews play
at the Bridge a few times. A couple of years later I
ended up playing against him. He was forty-nine but
Chooper Harris still kicked him. But what does stand
out from those days were the huge crowds. They gave
a real buzz to the place and there was always a
terrific atmosphere, without there ever being a hint
of trouble. I think the players were a lot closer to the
fans then. On the train home from away games we'd
go and have a beer with the supporters, talk about
the game and things like that. They were brilliant,
they really were. They went everywhere with us and
we got to know most of them; I suppose you could say
we all became friends. They used to ask us all what
we were doing after the game and we'd quite often
meet up on a Saturday night. There were certain
pubs down the King's Road that we used to use and
there would always be supporters in there.

This all helped the likes of me, Hutch and Huddie
develop an affinity for the club which I don't think
players have today, because they don't have that
level of contact with the supporters. They're too much
like film stars and they put barriers up round
themselves all the time, and keep away from 'the
people'. But we were just like ordinary blokes. It was

just a job for us. Now it's so high profile it's a totally different relationship. We knew who was paying our wages, it was the fans on the terraces.

One of the many perks of playing for Chelsea at that time was meeting Raquel Welch. Richard Attenborough – bless his heart, he's a lovely man and it's great to still see him at the club – was producing a new film starring Raquel. He told her about his love of Chelsea and she said she'd heard about Peter Osgood and wanted to meet me. Well, at least that's what Dickie told me, and I must say I'm quite happy to believe it.

The whole place was packed with celebrities in those days, much in the same way as it is now. The King's Road was buzzing. There was Carnaby Street, The Beatles and the Stones, and Chelsea were classed in the same category. We were all from the same mould so it was quite natural to see actors and pop stars at the ground.

I still love the club, there's no doubt about that. I still get a buzz just walking out on the pitch on a Saturday. In recent years I've supported them in Europe too, and I'm sure there's not many guys who can say they played for their club in one European cup final, and followed them across Europe to support them in another.

I just want to see them win things because I think the fans have waited for too long. Twenty-six years between trophies is ridiculous for a club like Chelsea.

And that's had a big effect on the players who were in those cup-winning teams in the early 1970s. Up until recently we were Chelsea's last successful team; we were a benchmark that people looked backed to and by which they measured success. We've been rammed down people's throats as the last team to win anything and that got up the noses of certain people in the boardroom. And sadly that led to us being resented at the club for a long time. There was the view that people had been looking back for too long, and you can't do that, you have to look forward. And I agreed with that but it was a bit embarrassing for us. We were the club's biggest fans not just because we love Chelsea but also because the more successful Chelsea are, the more work we get on TV, in the papers or doing speeches or whatever. So of course we wanted them to do well. We didn't want to be known as the last Chelsea team to win anything anymore than the directors did.

We were a close-knit team and we're still great mates. Ronnie rings me every day and I speak to Tommy Baldwin a lot. And of course Hutch has been my best friend in life, he's like a brother to me.

I never wanted to leave the club but Dave Sexton had made it clear that I didn't figure in his plans anymore. It was ridiculous the way it all ended. I went to see him and said I was willing to negotiate a new contract and stay at Stamford Bridge for the rest of my life. And he said, 'OK, I'll see the Chairman.'

But when I spoke to the Chairman three weeks later, he said, 'What contract? I don't know anything about it.' So that was me gone. I knew I couldn't play for Dave Sexton anymore. As it happens we're good friends now, and I'm sure we would both have done things differently had we had another chance. But that's the way it went, and that's life.

When Eddie McCreadie became the Chelsea manager me and Alan Hudson went up to the King's Road and had lunch with him one Wednesday. We'd heard he wanted to buy us back. I'd only been gone about six months and I just couldn't wait. Eddie was a good pal too but unfortunately it wasn't to be. In the end I had four or five great years at Southampton. Of course we won the FA Cup as well, which helped, and it was great to work under Lawrie McMenemy. Then I went off to the States for six months, but I didn't like it, so I came back and the first club I approached was Chelsea.

In retrospect, it was a mistake but then again it needn't have been. They put me straight back into the first team, which was wrong. I should have played in the reserves and worked with the kids. You know, just been on the fringes. We had a great reserve side then and I was enjoying every minute of it. It was good fun to play with the kids and see them come through, and they respected me. I even thought that perhaps I could have taken a coaching role and who knows, ultimately become manager. But then

Geoff Hurst arrived and that was it. Him and Bobby Gould, I couldn't play under those two. They weren't Chelsea for me, they really weren't. In the end I just said to Geoff Hurst, 'I'm going', and he said, 'Yeah, I've heard it before.' So I played on the Wednesday night against Oxford Reserves, picked my cards up on Thursday morning and left. It was a sad way to end things but I'm glad I did it then.

I was only thirty-two, but apart from football, the only skill I had was as a bricklayer, and the last thing I wanted to do was go on the building site. So I ended up buying a pub with Hutch in Old Windsor. I suppose it became a bit of a Chelsea shrine really. The word went out that we had a Sunday morning side, and teams used to queue up to play us in charity games, which was good for business too.

The really sad thing was that none of us went to see any games in those days because we knew we weren't welcome at Stamford Bridge. And there was no way I was going to pay to watch Chelsea Football Club. I'm not being funny or anything but I thought I deserved a little more than that after my years of service. To be honest, I don't think I'd ever pay to go and watch any club play. I knew people like Terry Venables, George Graham, Joe Royle and Harry Redknapp, and you've only got to ring them. I mean you don't abuse it, but they'll always be able to oblige you. So basically I ended going to see other teams more than I did Chelsea. But it wasn't through choice.

Gradually things changed though, peace was made and I've worked at the club for five years now doing PR. When Chelsea got through to the FA Cup Final against Manchester United I thought it was a great opportunity to finally bury the hatchet. Ken Bates had made a presentation on the pitch at Stamford Bridge with players from the 1970 team and everyone loved it. I thought the club should have invited all the old players back to Wembley as well. It would have been terrific. But at the end of the day he just wanted us to be forgotten and buried. It's just his way. Unfortunately they got beat 4–0 which made it even worse for us because we had to wait another three years before a new Chelsea side finally took the spotlight off us.

Nowadays what happens behind the scenes doesn't bother me. In fact I didn't even want to know what's going on. I'm just a Chelsea supporter. I just want to watch them play, do my PR thing and talk to other fans. My eldest son supports Southampton because he doesn't think Chelsea treated me too well, but the other two are both Chelsea. The youngest one is mad about them. He hasn't been to the Bridge yet but I've got him a shirt. Number nine with Osgood across the top. Now there's a thought.

Lance Percival

I don't know why but my visits to Chelsea have quite
often involved some kind of romantic entanglement.
In the days when the old East Stand used to have a
restaurant at the back, we always used to go there at
half-time to get a cup of tea or a stiff drink. I
remember once taking a girlfriend to watch
Sunderland play Chelsea. She'd never been to a
football match before. It was 0–0 at half-time and we
went for a drink, got talking and quite forgot about
the match until someone shouted that it was starting
again. So we rushed back to our seats and just as we
sat down a goal went in. So up jumped my girlfriend,
roaring and applauding but the rest of the stand was
absolutely silent because Sunderland had just taken
the lead. Not only had she not realized that the
teams had changed ends but she also thought
Chelsea were playing in red and white stripes!

Another dalliance occurred when I was on the

Blues Committee which raised money for the club
when we were in desperate circumstances, before
Ken Bates took over. This was in 1976 and people
were just trying to do their bit to keep the club from
going bankrupt. We had a bunch of business people
trying to do this, that and the other, and one of the
things we did was raise a couple of thousand quid
through a dance. My friend, who I had a season
ticket with, and I went to this dance together, but I
got talking to the girl he came with. We ended up
spending most of the evening together and we got on
so well that we got married in the end. Obviously this
didn't impress my friend too much and he went off to
live in Texas after that. But I don't think there were
too many hard feelings because he was actually
trying to take her sister out!

I don't expect too many people have met their
wives at a football ground, although I'm sure a few
marriages have broken up because of them. My wife
and I soon developed this unwritten rule that if she
didn't have to come and watch Chelsea then I didn't
have to go shopping. And that suited us both.

I've been a Chelsea supporter all my life although
I must admit to being a lapsed season ticket holder,
even though I only live a mile down the road. Not
that that means a lot because Chelsea has such a
strange base in terms of support. It has little to do
with the people that live in Chelsea at all. My
interest started when Dad took me, but this doesn't

happen with modern kids because they see teams on the TV before they go to a live game. My first memories of Chelsea are sitting on my father's shoulders in the Shed during the days of Roy Bentley in the fifties. I don't think anyone could get away with that now. You'd be told to piss off and get down in no uncertain times.

I've stood or sat in just about every part of the ground and I was actually going to Chelsea when the West Stand was being built. A whole gang of us used to go to matches in the sixties and I always remember when we came back, everybody used to sit in the car on the way home with their hands over their ear so they didn't hear the results and spoil *Match of the Day*. It must have looked a ridiculous sight, but the driver always insisted on keeping the radio on.

One of the great games I remember from around that time was Greaves' last before he left, when he scored four against Nottingham Forest. He was the cat's whiskers. Another game that particularly stands out is the League Cup Final against Leicester City in 1965. It was two legs in those days and I recall Eddie McCreadie dribbling the whole length of the pitch to score in the first game, which we won 3–2. Spurred on by this I drove up the motorway to see the second leg. I think it finished goalless but we'd done enough in the first game to win the cup. (It's always been interesting that we seem to be a lot better at winning cups than leagues, but I hope that will change now.) We joined up with the team when we got back that day. I knew them quite well, the Osgoods and the Cookes, players like that. I still run into Peter Osgood regularly.

I also remember one game back in the sixties, I think it was West Ham we were playing, and it finished 5–5. And the next day in the papers both managers complained about how dreadful their teams were playing and that things had got to improve. But this was exactly the type of game that we wanted to see.

When my son, Jamie, was about six I took him to see his first match but it was unfortunate timing because it was when we were fighting to hold on to a place in the First Division. I think we were playing Middlesborough in the play-offs. And as usual there was a string of expletives aimed at the referee which you wouldn't think twice about normally but I had a six-year-old asking me what they all meant. So that put the mockers on taking him at that stage. So I took Jamie to see Manchester United play, because he's a little traitor and he supported them then, although he's actually moved on to Arsenal now. But in the end it was Ken Bates who actually asked me to come back.

I won't be alone in nominating Charlie Cooke as my favourite player. His skill on the ball always made him a joy to watch. The same was true of

Jimmy Greaves. They had such individual skill. So did Hudson and Osgood, in different measures, but Cooke had that dribbling skill. Not necessarily in the Ryan Giggs style but drawing, swerving, moving in a very small space. Of the current team my favourite is Zola but like a lot of people I'm still to be convinced about this squad rotation thing. How do you get any cohesion? I always thought one of the secrets of a successful team was that one player always knew that so and so was going to be here or there to receive a pass.

Chelsea has certainly had its ups and downs but I think the new breed of supporters are a lot more demanding than we were in those days. If you've got great players you expect them to play well and ultimately for the club to win things. I think they've a better all-round team than they've ever had before. The 1970 team was of equal quality but it just didn't have the consistency to win the League.

Since I've taken up golf, I don't get to Chelsea as often as I did, but I always follow the results. My next door neighbour is Leslie Grantham and he goes to West Ham regularly. Luckily, honours are usually quite even between us and the Hammers.

Chelsea's always been a showbiz club, but no one on the *Carry On* cast was ever very interested in football. It's pretty hard to imagine Kenneth Williams standing in the Shed or Charles Hawtrey hurling abuse at the ref!

Adam Porter

I did the full twenty-five-year stretch. Condemned to
a quarter-century of footballing solitude. Forever
watching a parade of other teams hoist trophies
above their heads. Live it up on open-topped buses.
Embark on often successful European campaigns
whilst watching their fans generally having a big
party whilst drinking and often throwing about bits
of foreign soil. I wasn't allowed to play. Worst of all I
was banged up with my dad.

My dad first took me to football. I remember him
standing at the top of the stairs saying, 'Do you want
to go and watch the Blues?' I replied, 'Who are the
Blues?'

The trainspotters will want to know which game
it was, to verify correctness. It was when Harold
Wilson was Prime Minister. In fact he was there
being a Town fan. It was Chelsea v Huddersfield, 5
January 1972. The score was 2–2. It was about seven

months after Chelsea had won the European Cup
Winners' Cup in Athens against Real Madrid. If you
had told me aged seven that it would be 1997 before
we would win anything again I might have
reconsidered my position.

My dad moved in with me and my mum when I
was five and out again when I was eleven. The
product of an illicit affair, I was splurged whilst my
dad was still married to someone else. People think
the sixties were all about beards and beads, but my
mum had to flee her native North London in case
anyone wondered where that ugly lump under her
arm had come from. Women were still taken for
granted, sexual liberation brought with it a section of
people who couldn't react to its full implications.
Things like long-term responsibility hadn't occurred
to them yet. It was just another way that men could
have a field day. So, cohabiting with dad was
something I can barely remember. Going to football
with him was different.

He was an irritable, dominating man capable of
extreme ebullience, much charm and great material
generosity who loved me to bits, mainly because I
was a boy and an inappropriately titled 'lovechild'. A
more capable and interested mind than mine could
probably piece together the rites and rituals that led
me to overtake my dad in terms of fanaticism for
Chelsea within weeks. Even though I didn't go to the
1972 League Cup Final I actually cried when I saw

the result on the news. Even I find that puzzling.
What sort of daft bloody child was that? I had only
gone to the match twice by then? What desperate act
of wanting to belong made me weep at something I
could only have had a fleeting association with?
Soppy twat.

Of course, I ended up a bit like my dad, but then
again a bit different. I was physically violent.
Football's actual and implicit violence fascinated me.
I can remember being so terrified at Chelsea-Millwall
games that the whole world seemed to be on fire.
These big grown men fighting everywhere. But I
understate it. It wasn't just Chelsea-Millwall. Those
days, the seventies and early eighties, it was every
week. One of my first memories of Chelsea is Dad
picking me up and running from West Ham after a
3–1 defeat (Bill Garner's home début if I remember
well enough). He had me under his arm and I was
facing behind him as we legged it. I could see the
street seemed to be full of claret and blue and young
men scaring people and singing. As I got older I
began to escape my dad's grasp, running off at the
final whistle to get as close (or occasionally, when I
got it wrong, actually in) to the violence as I could.
Because, like the rest of the fans at the time, I grew
to understand hate, who to hate, where and how. You
know, male role models and all. Sometimes he would
try and stop me. Sometimes he would make me sit
down as a torrent of disgusting abuse poured forth

aimed at the opposition, usually their fans. I
remember him restraining me aged twelve when
fighting broke out in the East Stand during the
memorable 4–2 FA Cup win over Liverpool. I wanted
to join in. But he hardly ever told me off. I could
scare my dad at football. I knew more about it, felt it
more. It made me powerful. Over him too.

One of the only times he ever hit me was at
football. I racially abused Laurie Cunningham when
he was playing for Orient, ripping Chelsea to pieces.
My dad dragged me out of the seats and took me
about five steps down into the stand and began to
hit me, I was about eleven. He was screaming at me.
He was Jewish after all. He had escaped from
Frankfurt late on in 1939 and he couldn't handle
racism. Neither can I. Even at that age I already
knew what I was doing was wrong. In his later years
I became far more left-wing than him, chastising his
inability to think things through to logical
conclusions. Also, Laurie Cunningham became my
favourite ever non-Chelsea player. I still have some
video of him taking corners for Real Madrid. He
used to take them with the outside of either foot and
whip them in like a viper's sting. He had Cali Cartel
assassins in his boots, that man. I cried when he
died. So, what does that make me? A respecter of
violence? A stupid child caught up in hatred and
partisanship? A closet racist? Or was that one of the
very few lessons I had from him, a kid eager to learn

about how to be a bloke? That particular one seemed to stick.

But there were a lot of tense days at the Bridge. Dad knew nothing about football. The details seemed stupid to him. He had not been brought up in the UK so perhaps he missed the identification that I found almost immediately. I felt accepted at Chelsea, especially away from home. I was anonymous. Half Jew, half Prot, half middle-class half working-class. Shit in class. Fuck it, it didn't matter. Chelsea and my mates from school accepted me. Like the foreign legion. But just at weekends.

Yes, there were many great adventures to be had as a marauding youth and a great sport to watch as well. Albeit over the twenty-five years played in the most part at Chelsea by a bunch of fucking prats.

We used to argue like hell at times. Mainly when Chelsea were doing badly. He couldn't understand what football was about. He had never played it as a kid. I did. I played about eight years for the school and then some afterwards. Still do. He came to watch my début and that was it. When I pestered my mum to run a Sunday team he sometimes used to come down and watch. The only time he was any use was when the much harder Paddington Boys' Club tried to fight us before the game. He threatened them. They could have had him though, shitters.

As we got older we did do some different things. But mainly over our lives we must have spent so much time going to, coming from or at football as to be untrue. When Chelsea came up from the five-year stint in Division Two, where our devotion to the old season ticket was sorely tested, we went to the away game at Portsmouth together. He never travelled away with Chelsea. Even QPR seemed too far. I ended up protecting him, a slightly frail sixty-year-old, as the final whistle was greeted with a tirade of violence in and around the ground. Of course he still found time to chastise a policeman trying to arrest some Chelsea. 'Fucking pigs, those people are fucking pigs, like the fucking gestapo,' he used to say. I loved that. When he was jabbing his finger into the chest of a frightened officer on the Fratton Park terraces, the fans were singing (topically at the time) 'Libyans are our friends, they kill coppers.' It all made perfect, beautiful sense to me. I was probably more proud of him at that moment than I ever was. My dad at the front of a baying mob of Chelsea, we had finally become . . . well . . . sort of British, we did belong somewhere. However, had my Dad been able to decipher the chant the same would not have been true. His later years were marked with an unpleasant racism (actually enthicism) towards Arabs. I refer you to my comment about 'thinking things through' above. Still, you don't . . . er . . . think about things like that at the time.

My dad was in fact superb at being completely oblivious to the extremes of racism that were so

prevalent at Chelsea in those days. As 'Spurs are on
their way to Auschwitz' was sung by half the ground,
dad would be picking his nose or something, reading
the programme and tutting at the poor English. I
swear he never heard that chant. Because when he
did hear it he would respond. 'Like a Yid that's
standing on a five pence piece, we shall not be moved'
sang some sad boot-boys – I was already a soulboy –
in the queue to get in one time. He started on them
all, I tried to look like I could have all ten of them.
But they shat their pants like Paddington Boys' Club
and I didn't get a big hiding. Maybe it was the
same guys?

When he got to seventy, going to the Bridge
became too much for him. Generally a disciple of the
East Stand, he could no longer climb the many steps
to the upper tier and couldn't see anything either. He
was very pleased at the fact that Sky TV showed
some Chelsea games at my house so he could still see
what was happening. I remember us sitting in the
West Stand (the 'less steps' theory) when Darren
Barnard scored against West Ham in a 2–0 win. He
said 'I can't see what's going on' after about twenty
minutes. I could see him getting old. I could measure
it against Stamford Bridge, also Wembley. I got him
a ticket for the 1994 Cup semi-final against Luton.
He had to listen to the radio through the game to
know what was up because he was so far from the
pitch he had no hope of seeing anything. I wasn't

sitting with him, but I kept an eye. He looked small
and vulnerable at Wembley amongst the celebrating
hordes. White-haired, fat, but slow and arthritic. But
then he drained my sympathy as only he knew how.
As we came out he called a bunch of Chelsea fans
'fucking morons' within earshot for doing something
like singing loudly. He was pissed off that he couldn't
get his way (in this case participate in the
celebrations) so he took it out on someone.

At Gullit's first game I thought he was going to
die. The draw with Everton was on a very hot day
and his shirt was soaked and he was passing
out/falling asleep in the seat. After the game I had to
go and get his car (like an idiot he drove until he was
almost blind) and take it through the police cordon as
my mate Zaki waited with him outside the Black
Bull. Those occasions became more frequent.

Then one day he couldn't see Sky either.
December 1996. We lost, as always, away at Leeds,
2–0 this time. Chelsea were shit that day, Gullit as
manager or not. I told Dad to shut-up a couple of
times when he was going off on one about how shit
Chelsea always were. It used to irritate me, we were
shit but he never got the right reasons, he just liked
to shoot off at the mouth. But that day he couldn't
even see the TV and I had him sat right slap-bang in
front of it. I had to take him home and perform the
painful ritual of helping him slowly up the stairs to
his flat. That was the last I saw of him alive. He died

three days after that, and when Roberto Di Matteo
scored after forty-three seconds at Wembley six
months later, I missed him a lot. Fuck you Chelsea,
you tardy playboy twats. You were six months late.
And I thought you cared.

Steven Redgrave

I first became interested in Chelsea during the late sixties. My schoolfriends were all into football and everybody had their teams and for some reason, I really don't know why, I tagged on to Chelsea. But then I discovered rowing, and like most people who get very involved in another sport, I found making the time to watch football very difficult. I've not seen Chelsea live that often because when I started rowing we used to race every Saturday, and then as a senior Saturday was always a very big training day. So most of my supporting has really been done through Teletext, which I can assure you is the most nerve-racking way to follow a game of football.

I do manage to go now and again, particularly to midweek games, and I was lucky enough to be out in Seville on a training camp last year when we played

Betis, so I got to see that game. I spend about twenty weeks away from home every year, but I'll certainly go more often when I finally get round to retiring.

Living in Marlow I was very tempted to go to the Oxford FA Cup game this season but the fact that it was on TV proved too much in the end, I'm afraid. One particular FA Cup game I remember was against Newcastle United in the third round a few years ago, but I had a better excuse for not going that time – I was in Australia. The first game was a draw at Stamford Bridge and the replay went back up north, but keeping up with events was proving very difficult. It was the morning out in Australia when the game was going on and I ran back from training to find out the result. I phoned my wife and she said it had gone into extra-time, and when I phoned again it had gone to penalties. Then she phoned back to give me a blow-by-blow account of the shoot-out – they were probably the most expensive penalties ever taken.

People quite often ask me which sportsmen or women are the fittest and when I was younger I'd always maintained that rowers were. However, now I'm a bit older and a little bit more mature, I just concentrate on being fit within my own sport. Different activities require different levels of fitness. People try rowing and find it very hard but if I was to play football and run round like a headless chicken for ninety minutes I'd get pretty tired as well. So I avoid judging my sport against others. Mind you, when I came third in the last-ever series of *Superstars* I can't remember too many footballers doing that well. In fact, a swimmer called Robin Brew won it, and Joe Lydon, the Rugby League player, was second. But if I had to pick anyone from the Chelsea team to be in a boat with me then Zola would be the natural choice for a cox because he's so small, and given the size of De Goey, I think he'd make a pretty good stroke.

When I was kid I used to play in goal, so Peter Bonetti was my schoolboy hero although, of course, I also like Osgood. We still have a bit of kick-about at training camps, just for some light-hearted fun while we're away, although getting a group of rowers to play football is always very amusing because normally the reason people take up rowing is because they're crap at every other sport.

Things are certainly changing at Stamford Bridge, but all Chelsea supporters are still wary of the fact that we can play the best team in the world one week, and hold our heads up high, yet the following week play a team from a much lower division and perform terribly.

One of my little girls, who's seven, is now taking an interest and has got all that to look forward to. But my son is only nine months old. He's got some Chelsea slippers but that's as far as it goes – at the moment.

Giles Smith

For nearly a quarter of a century, supporting Chelsea
was a reliably miserable experience – something akin
to repeatedly slamming your fingers in a filing
cabinet. Right now, from where I sit (Matthew
Harding Stand, Upper Tier), it's in grave danger
of becoming a pleasure. Friends, these are
worrying times.

Three trophies in two seasons; five Wembley
appearances in four years; an ever-expanding squad
of players made up almost entirely of glossy
continental thoroughbreds; a spanking new state-of-
the-art stadium; sell-out crowds; the availability at
half-time of smoked salmon and cream cheese bagels,
blueberry muffins and an amusingly drinkable little
cup of white coffee – such is life at Chelsea at the end
of the century. Who would have thought it? In July of
1998, two members of the squad were all over the
television kissing the World Cup and waving their

winners' medals around. Yes, that's two members of
a Chelsea squad. Is it any wonder some of us don't
quite know where we are?

During France 98, I heard a commentator talking
about Brian Laudrup. And what the commentator
said was, '. . . the Chelsea man – showing he can live
with the Brazilians. . . .' These were not words I ever
expected to hear spoken – unless by someone who was
either drunk or mad or both. I followed Chelsea
through the doggedly featureless years of the
seventies and eighties. Back then, the only way a
Chelsea player was going to live with Brazilians was
by emigrating. And on some of the darker afternoons
when Gareth Hall was playing, I knew many people
who would have organized a whip-round for the fare.
From Gareth Hall to Brian 'living with the Brazilians'
Laudrup: this is how far things have come.

The last time Chelsea were anywhere near this
interesting, it was 1970, they had just won the FA
Cup and I was eight. That's where I came in. Their
success was magnetic and the future looked bright.
Two years and one European trophy later, it all
started to fall apart. And we, the new intake, were
stranded in the rubble. There were thousands of us
out there. To use a metaphor from the modern game,
we invested heavily in the club in the boom years and
then watched, ashen-faced, as the line indicating the
value of our shares turned abruptly downward and
fell off the bottom of the graph.

Here's what the next twenty years or so brought us: dire trophylessness; periodic spells in the Second Division; one stomach-churning flirtation with relegation to the Third; non-stop crowd mayhem; threats of electric fences; imminent financial disaster; Mickey Droy. True, there was a brief period of excellence under John Neal – the Nevin-Dixon-Speedie years. But even that didn't lead to major honours, and the old grinding rhythm soon re-established itself. Chelsea under Ian Porterfield were so exhaustingly grim and meaningless, it drove me and my friend Ben to gambling. We would put a quid on Mal Donaghy (a centre back, not famous for imaginative forays into the penalty area, and thus commonly available at around 60–1) to score, just so we had the pleasure of shouting 'Have a dig, Mal' every time he got the ball. In those days, it was the only way we knew to keep ourselves awake.

But then enter Glenn Hoddle, and then Ruud Gullit, and then Gianluca Vialli, and suddenly it's all silverware and flair and silky Italians. For my generation, this is hard to get used to. And sometimes, when I am leaving the ground after another six-goal victory, I look around me at the small children, skipping towards the exits in the gentle evening sunlight, with their replica shirts and their Zola flags and their big smiles, and I am filled with the urge to lead them aside for a moment, prod them into the shadow of the Chelsea Hotel, and say,

'Listen, sonny: it wasn't always like this, you know.'

Anyone who took up with Chelsea in the seventies knows all about deprived formative years. But I like to think my own childhood with the club was, in some respects, uniquely barren. It was ages before I got to see them play at all, let alone play well. For something like six years, I supported Chelsea sight unseen. I grew up maybe seventy miles away from the ground in Colchester, Essex. My parents were not remotely enthusiastic about football. And they were even less enthusiastic about allowing their son to disappear off to London on his own to watch it. I had plotted the journey to Stamford Bridge a thousand times, using the map of the London Underground at the back of an old Lett's diary: the train to Liverpool Street and then round on the green line to Fulham Broadway. But if I had conceived a plan to go on a solo cycling holiday through war-torn Afghanistan, it would have been more positively received. In the dark ages of the seventies, power cuts and hooliganism were all the rage. Permission was never granted.

I suppose I should be glad to reflect that my parents liked me enough not to want me to get mugged on a Tube train by West Ham fans; and, in fairness to them, the papers and television news bulletins at this time tended to support their hunch by regularly publishing documentary evidence of the dangers of football attendance. Pictures of fans with

darts in their foreheads, images of smouldering train
carriages – that kind of thing. But at the time my
parents' caution seemed to me to be merely irksome.
I don't recall expressing any gratitude to them for it.

Strangely, though, this deprivation had a kind of
hothouse effect. Fed intensively at home on
magazines, newspaper cuttings and old programmes,
my relationship with Chelsea grew to develop many
of the attributes of a successful, long-term marriage.
It had passion, commitment, concern and deep
knowledge – or certainly on my part. But no actual
football. No substantial contact with the club of any
kind, really. Just hearsay and rumour and long
Saturday afternoons spent wondering how Chelsea
were getting on, and desperate surrogates for a
genuine, hands-on encounter.

For instance, the elderly lady who lived in the
bungalow over the road (she was known,
mysteriously, as Aunty Bill) had a friend who worked
in a post office and sweet shop on the Fulham Road.
And into this post office would come – or so Bill said
– Alan Hudson and Peter Osgood and Charlie Cooke,
among others. I was breathless with excitement
when I heard this. I felt that, at a stroke, it brought
me somehow nearer the club: I knew someone who
knew someone who was in contact on a day-to-day
basis with key Chelsea personnel. Well, maybe not
day-to-day. I don't know how often the backbone of
Chelsea's trophy-winning early seventies side visited

this post office. It didn't occur to me to ask. About as often as they needed stamps, I guess. And I don't know, either, whether they came in all together or separately, though, in the many hours I spent poring over this fascinating nugget of information, I assumed the former. Naive of me, I now see. But these were, in some ways, more innocent times in which to have been a fan; and more innocent times, too, in which to have been running a post office and sweet shop. These days there would be a hand-written sign on the door saying, 'Only two unaccompanied FA Cup winners at a time'.

According to Bill's friend, Cooke, Hudson, Osgood and the rest were 'right lads'. Bill told me this in her bungalow one day, with a playful half-smile and an arch of the eyebrow, and I imagine I smiled back and arched one of my eyebrows too, though, being only eight, I hadn't got a clue what she was on about. But I think even then, drunk as I was with fascination, I realized that Bill's inside information hardly amounted to a dazzling tabloid exclusive. ('Chelsea Heroes Are "Right Lads" – Shock Claim of Friend of Someone Who Served Them in Post Office, Possibly More Than Once.')

If you had witnessed the strength and blind persistence of my determination to get to Stamford Bridge, you would have backed me to get there eventually – though it was typical of the early years of my attachment to Chelsea that my first visit to the ground should have taken place shortly after dawn and during the close season. The visit took place in 1975, when I was thirteen. I was going on holiday to Cornwall with my parents. We were driving, so I put it to my father (several times and on several occasions) that maybe we could call in at Stamford Bridge on the way.

My father was sceptical at first. This was some years before the M25 London Orbital, but even then, you didn't need to be Christopher Columbus to realize that the most direct route from Colchester to Padstow did not go via the Fulham Road. Yet my persistence must have worn him down, because my father eventually agreed that we would make a detour. It warms my heart now to think I had the kind of parents who would put themselves out for their son in this way. That said, they didn't act entirely out of altruism; they would have foreseen something in it for themselves, too. They were hoping I would shut up.

Assuming we set off from Essex at about five in the morning, and remembering that my father was a fairly cautious driver, I estimate that we would have reached the bottom of the Fulham Road at about seven. My father pulled over opposite the main gate, alongside where a pair of phoneboxes now sits and where people park their bikes on matchdays. There were no bikes or people around on this occasion, nor any traces, really, of the thrilling colour and noise

that, I imagined, would fill a mid-season Saturday
afternoon. But that's because it was seven o'clock in
the morning in July.

Yet here I was at the very gates, the sun was
shining, and it felt good. That said, there was a
pretty drastic limit to what I could now do. The club
shop wasn't open. The forecourt was not throbbing
with chairmen and members of the board. Nor even
cleaning staff. And it was too early for Peter Osgood
to be out buying stamps. (If he was half the 'right lad'
people were claiming, he was probably just getting
ready for bed.) Nevertheless, clutching a freshly
loaded Kodak Instamatic, I crossed the road and took
two commemorative pictures.

One showed the turnstiles – heavily locked and
boarded at this point – which used to allow access to
the Shed, with the side of what was then the new
East Stand bulking above them. (It is some indication
of the developmental torpor which descended on
Stamford Bridge that people were still referring to it
as 'the new East Stand' some 20 years later.) The
other picture was of a sign saying 'Visiting
Supporters: Use Other End of Ground', beneath which
someone had written 'West Ham'. Once they were
developed, I was to file these rather undistinguished
yet, for me, utterly totemic images in the plastic-
pocketed leaves of a green photo-album from Boots
with a weirdly spongy cover, where they remain to
this day: a rather odd intrusion in an otherwise

seamless parade of poor quality beach shots, wildly optimistic pictures of a duck which landed in our garden for a few hours and many images of my family eating things in outdoor locations.

The visit had taken, at most, three minutes. Having done what I needed to do, and with one last lingering look in the direction of the boarded-up turnstiles, I got back into the car and we set off again in the direction of Cornwall. I'm not sure this pilgrimage to Stamford Bridge meant quite as much to my parents as it did to me. Neither of them got out to have a look or even to stretch their legs. I'm pretty sure my father left the car's engine running. But, as I settled back into my seat for the remainder of the nineteen-hour drive (or however long it was), I experienced a sense of relaxation and fulfilment which the following fortnight was never going to come close to reproducing. For me the vacation was already over. I had got the holiday snaps I wanted.

Those photographs tided me over for another year, until I finally got to return to Chelsea in glory. On a Saturday. During the football season. When they were at home. I had been siphoning off some of the frustration in the meantime by going to watch Colchester United, a side of dubious merit who, on the rare occasions when they weren't in the Fourth Division, were busy being relegated from the Third. This my parents did not consider dangerous. Quite rightly. And I did not consider it football. I suppose

I was mildly involved, in a curious sort of way. And I
did collect the autographs of Colchester United
players (Mike Walker, Mickey Cook, Steve Foley),
but only on a casual basis and for the same reason
that people climb mountains: because they were
there. I knew all along that I would never take up
with Colchester United professionally. It was just a
way of keeping my hand in until the call came
from Chelsea.

And the call did finally come, courtesy of a
schoolfriend called Colin Saville and his dad, called
Mr Saville. Colin had one of those miracle fathers
who was prepared to take his son – not often, but
occasionally – to Stamford Bridge at times other than
7.00 a.m. in July. And on one of those occasions,
Colin invited me along. The date: 28 August 1976.
The match: Chelsea v Carlisle. Not exactly top-
ranking opposition, I admit, but this was during one
of Chelsea's semi-regular furloughs in the Second
Division and beggars can't be choosers. We did the
journey I knew so well, even though I had never done
it: the train to Liverpool Street and then round on
the green line to Fulham Broadway. Outside the
station, rain fell on us and continued to fall for the
rest of the afternoon. Unconcerned, we bought
enamel badges in the old souvenir shop, just along
the street from the Broadway. Then we passed
through the turnstiles at the Shed End and climbed
the steps beyond, where, nearly rigid with

excitement, I glimpsed the inside of that rattled old oval bowl for the first time. Once Colin and Mr Saville had finished putting my jaw back in place, we found a crush barrier to stand against, halfway down, to the right of the Shed.

Of the game which followed, I remember absolutely nothing. I have no memory of the goals. I know they were scored by Steve 'Jock' Finnieston and Kenny Swain, but that's because I just looked it up in my copy of *Chelsea: A Complete Record 1905–1991* by Scott Cheshire. But I could not tell you how the goals came about, nor even at which end of the ground they were scored. I do dimly recall that Chelsea were in blue, but knowledge might be supplementing experience here. I'd hazard a guess, similarly, that they played about forty-five minutes per half. Football-wise, the afternoon is a total blank.

So what do I remember? I remember that I wore a blue, plastic rain-top. (The word I am trying to avoid here is 'kaghoul'. It was not a kaghoul. It was a blue plastic rain-top.) I remember that I kept my programme in the blue, plastic rain-top's zippered front pocket. (I was neurotically concerned to get the programme home undamaged; but that's a story for another time and another psychotherapist.) I remember the scarves and singing from the centre of the Shed. (I probably spent as much time craning round to watch the centre of the Shed as I spent watching the game.) I remember a section of Carlisle fans at the far end of the ground, getting miserably wet. (Was there any ground in the world that provided a less hospitable environment for away supporters than Stamford Bridge in the seventies and eighties? Our guests were shown through to a wide swathe of crumbling terrace, made from communist-standard concrete, penned in at the front and entirely without shelter. If they were lucky, someone would come and poke a selection of low-quality snacks through the railings. It's amazing anyone ever came back.) I remember that 'Howzat' by Sherbet was played over the tannoy at half-time. And I remember wanting – quite against the odds, now that I think about it – to come again.

Also, I remember that Chelsea were 2–0 up with five minutes to go when Mr Saville did something for which I have never forgiven him. He decided we were leaving. Either he or Colin tapped me on the shoulder and when I turned to look, the pair of them were threading their way through the crowd along the crush-barrier and then setting off up the gangway. This was extraordinary behaviour. The game hadn't finished. What were they playing at? I wondered for a moment whether they were involved in some elaborate practical joke at my expense. When I realized, with dismay, that they weren't, I set off after them.

You just don't know with some people. I had assumed, on that afternoon in 1976, that I was in the guardianship of a gentle and generous man whose nomination for a 'Dad of the Year' award I would have been only too happy to second. Only now did he reveal himself to be one of those 'leave early and beat the rush' maniacs. True, as I would later come to know, if you stay to the end at Stamford Bridge, you stand the chance of becoming one of maybe 15,000 people trying to make their way through a twelve-foot gate into the Tube station. You may have to take your place in the heavily policed crush which builds up along the Fulham Road while the blockage slowly clears. And for some of that wait, you may well find your face squashed against the flank of a police horse. But you will have missed nothing of the game – and what's a little discomfort and a moment of unexpected intimacy with a highly trained gelding in comparison with that certain knowledge?

Because, of course, while we were jogging down the Fulham Road in the rain that day, Carlisle took it upon themselves to tuck away a late consolation goal. Now, obviously I would have been more ruined had Chelsea scored. Yet the incompleteness of the experience on this, my first time, rankled for months. We didn't know that the scoreline had changed until someone with a radio on the train to Colchester happened to mention it, about an hour later. Here was high irony. I had assumed that those long Saturday afternoons of wondering how Chelsea were getting on would come to an end once I actually started going to the games; as someone in the ground, I was expecting to be in a pretty good position to know how they were doing. But no.

Still, there was a lesson to be learned here. Walking out is all very well in the intervals at theatres or during musical concerts. But you don't do it at football. These days, I get to control my own destiny in this respect. When the old West Stand was pulled down, the beautiful vindication of democracy-in-action which is the ballot system delivered me to the front row of the Matthew Harding Upper. I occupy that seat for the full ninety, and for the most part, I am very happy to be there – if slightly bewildered and suspicious, and with dark urges to start lecturing the nearby youngsters, like an old man with his memories of the war.

Take my own son, for instance. He's growing up in South London, not far over the river from the ground. Whether he likes it or not (and he's too young yet to have thought much about it) Chelsea are his local team. Not for him some six years of pent up misery plotting imaginary journeys with the London Underground map in the back of an old diary. Not for him the meagre satisfactions of second-hand gossip from some so-called Aunty Bill. He could be hands-on with Chelsea as soon as he's likely to enjoy it. What age would that be? Four? Five? It's up to him, but he could be looking at being a season-ticket holder by the time he's seven. Seven! What's more, he was delivered at the Chelsea & Westminster hospital in Fulham Road in a delivery room which offered a panoramic view of Stamford Bridge. Four days later Chelsea won the FA Cup.

Kids today: they don't know they're born.

Francis Wheen

Football supporters, by and large, are a loyal bunch. Like the club itself, they're a constant. Players on the other hand come and go, but while they're at the club we expect them to give their all and take things as seriously as we do. Anyway, my eyes were opened to the world of professional footballers late last year. It was a strange experience really, in fact something that in retrospect was quite disgraceful. I was having dinner at the House of Commons with a MP friend on the eve of our defeat against Wimbledon in the Worthington Cup. I was waiting for him in the Central Lobby when all of a sudden Frank Leboeuf appeared – apparently he was having dinner with Tony Banks. Anyway, we ended up sitting at the table next to theirs. Obviously I was very happy about this, but I found myself thinking, 'Christ, shouldn't he be tucked up in bed with a mug of Ovaltine or something?' It was getting quite late by then and he had a very important match the next day. I didn't think it was right.

At 10 o'clock Banks had to go and vote, so I took the opportunity to introduce myself to Leboeuf. Now the dining-room is meant to be no smoking but Leboeuf took out a fag and lit up. The waiters were so overawed they didn't dare stop him. So I said, 'Surely you're meant to be playing tomorrow evening – this is no way to carry on'. He claimed he wasn't and as for the smoking he replied, 'Ah yes, we at Chelsea are not a drinking side, we are a smoking side,' as if that made it any better!

So I thought no more of it until the next night when, sure enough, there he was playing – and he had a disaster including giving away the penalty. He made a lot of uncharacteristic mistakes throughout the game and I thought, 'Hah, it's all because he was up late last night with fucking Banks.' So I hold Banks personally responsible for that defeat.

I suppose I first started supporting Chelsea in the winter of 1966, which of course was very good timing because they got to the FA Cup a few months later. There was an indirect family connection through my godfather Peter Jack, who worked for BOAC (the forerunner of British Airways) and lived just off the King's Road. He had a season ticket but his job meant he travelled a lot, so when he discovered I was now supporting Chelsea, he offered it to me when he was away. I lived in Kent then but from the age of about ten I used to make my way to Stamford Bridge on the train. Peter used to leave his ticket under the doormat. It was in the old West Stand although I'd also stand in the Shed if I hadn't got the ticket. Occasionally my father came with me especially if we were playing Manchester United, who my brother had decided to support.

When I was at boarding school we were allowed to watch *The Big Match* on a Sunday afternoon and I'm sure I saw Chelsea a few times, but I don't remember any great moment when I suddenly decided that I supported Chelsea. I liked the way they played; they were an attractive team and I had a friend, Jonathan Barker, who decided he was a Chelsea fan as well, so we kind of egged each other on a bit. We would obsessively compare the merits of Eddie McCreadie and John Hollins, and things like that.

I was into collecting things about the club too, largely because it was used as an inducement by my parents to make me behave at school. I was bone idle most of the time and used to get terrible reports. I remember after one of these reports, I was in WH Smiths in Bromley with my mother and there was this book by Ralph Finn called *A History of Chelsea FC* on the shelf. My mother saw me eyeing it up and said, 'Right, if you get a good report at the end of next term, you can have the book as a present. But you've got to behave.' It was sound psychology but she blew it really by buying the book there and then, so I knew

I'd get it eventually. But I did make a real effort not to get in trouble that term.

I also used to collect programmes, and not just from the games I went to. Our local team, Bromley, had about three supporters but amazingly enough it had a little shop in the ground which sold old programmes, and very good ones at that. So when I couldn't afford to go to Chelsea I'd pay a visit to Bromley, get in for about a penny and then, having saved up all my pocket money, I'd go and buy up all these old programmes at half-time. It wasn't just Chelsea ones, although of course they were a priority. I kept them for ages but annoyingly, in a moment of madness about ten years ago I gave them to Phil Shaw, the football correspondent on the *Independent*. I've regretted it ever since. My then wife was complaining about them taking up too much space and I happened to ask Phil whether he knew anyone who would be interested in a load of old programmes. He said he was and I handed them all over to him.

I used to get all the football magazines, like *Shoot!* and *Goal* and I seem to remember something called *Jimmy Hill's Soccer Weekly*, or something like that. There was one particular column, in *Shoot!* I think it was, written by Michael Wale (who later went on to do local news programmes on TV). When I was ten years old I thought his column was the finest, wittiest journalism I'd ever read in my life and reading it was the highlight of my week. I did all the

usual stuff like cutting out pictures and keeping
scrapbooks, although I don't know where they've
gone. But it did become quite obsessive and it went
beyond Chelsea. At one point I actually complied a
whole scrapbook grandly called 'The Latter Stages of
the Home Internationals'. It wasn't even about the
whole tournament. I must have laboriously collected
every report from every paper I could find just
covering the last few games.

Charlie Cooke was my big Chelsea hero. In games
at school that's who I always wanted to be. I used to
study him during matches and look at his boots to try
and work out what make they were, how he did his
laces, and how he had the tongues pulled up. I'd then
try and wear my football boots as close as possible to
how he wore them, and embark on these dribbles
down the wing although rarely with anything like the
success the real Charlie Cooke enjoyed.

There was an advertising campaign for eggs at
the time, encouraging you to eat them for breakfast.
It went, 'E for B' – which was eggs for breakfast –
'and be your best'. Manchester United changed it to,
'E for B, and Georgie Best', and then for some
perverse reason Chelsea fans started singing, 'E for
B, and Charlie Cooke', which completely missed the
point and the fact that the pun was on the word 'best'.

What stopped me going to Chelsea for a while was
a similar experience to that of David Mellor –
violence, although he went to Craven Cottage for a

couple of years which I drew the line at. There are
limits after all. It was an incident in 1978 that really
did it. I went down to Stamford Bridge with a friend
of mine called Clare Lovell, who was a Chelsea fan.
At that time you had to run the gauntlet of people
selling *National Front News* and *Bulldog*, and there
were some skinheads outside who asked Clare if she
wanted to buy a copy of *Bulldog* and she said no
thanks. So they asked why and she said she didn't
like the National Front and this torrent of abuse
came out. Suddenly we were surrounded by this gang
of hulking great skinheads pushing us around.
Luckily at that point a couple of policemen wandered
over and we didn't actually get beaten to a pulp.
There was so much racism down in the Shed it was
just awful and I got fed up with the whole thing.

Of course this did all coincide with a period when,
quite frankly, Chelsea weren't the most exciting team
in the country. It was a terrible dark age. True, it
was a hard act to follow because the previous side
had, to me, all been giants of the game. It was partly
that they didn't seem to have the same calibre of
player, although Mickey Droy, and Ray Wilkins
briefly, were entertaining, but also that the glamour
had gone. You can actually picture members of
Sexton's great team in nightclubs and buying natty
suits in the King's Road. They didn't seem out of
place, just like Vialli and co. today. But it's not as
easy to visualise Ian Britton shopping at Armani, or

Graham Wilkins popping into Vidal Sasson's.

By the mid-eighties I tentatively tried going back, but then, almost immediately I moved out to Oxfordshire when I got married and then children came along and we moved to rural Essex. The other thing that puts me off now is that you can no longer go to a game on the spur of the moment.

I have long chats with Andy Hamilton about Chelsea because one thing I'm hopeless at is knowing what has become of old players. Quite often I'll mention one of these players to Andy and he always seems to know what happened to them In fact he's usually had a drink with him the night before. Bobby Tambling was one. I'm sure I read he'd become a Jehovah's Witness and tried to convert other people and I think another Chelsea player joined as well. But I haven't heard about him since. I remember hearing rumours in the Shed that the club weren't very happy because they were afraid he was going to convert the whole team, because once you become a Jehovah's Witness it is your duty to convert other people. Perhaps they thought all the players were going to jack in football and spend their Saturday afternoons knocking on front doors instead.

One strange thing about football is the fuss people make if a footballer has actually got any qualifications to his name. In magazines like *Shoot!* they always used to refer to these players as the Professor or the Boffin even if they only had a low

second in Business Studies from some second-rate
Polytechnic, and on the strength of this he was
regarded as Renaissance Man. Pat Nevin was seen
like that and of course he had the punk music
knowledge, too. Graeme Le Saux came along as the
Guardian-reading footballer, although of course he's
far from the typical *Guardian*-reader on the pitch. He
behaves more like Vinny Jones. Why does he go so
berserk? It's quite a recent thing really – he's got
worse in the last year.

Just before Christmas last year I was desperate
to see the first of the two Chelsea games against
Manchester United, but that night I ended up at the
Foreign Office with Robin Cook. It was terrible. He
was having his Christmas party for the hacks but I'd
had a message saying could I come along half an
hour early because he wanted to have a private chat.
When I arrived he was on the phone to Madeleine
Albright (the US Secretary of State) so I sat waiting
for him and kept asking people whether the Foreign
Office had Sky or not. It was so frustrating because I
thought I was going to be able to get away and find
some bar to watch the game in but then America
went and bombed Iraq. I was stuck in the Foreign
Office until about one in the morning. They kept
saying, 'The Prime Minister's making a statement
from Downing Street and all you can worry about is a
bloody football match.' It didn't really seem worth
arguing that it wasn't just any football match.

Jimmy White

There are a lot of big football fans on the snooker circuit, but as far as I know, I'm the only Chelsea supporter. All the others go to Manchester United because they can blag free tickets. I like to pay for myself, although I'm hoping to get something for doing this piece for the book!

I was at Old Trafford when we beat United 2–0 a few years ago. I was sitting with John Virgo, who's a big Red, and when we scored I jumped and gave it some, even though I was in the United end. You know, just like anyone would have done. You just get carried away with it all and forget where you are, don't you? Anyway, all these pissed off United fans started shouting at Virgo for bringing a Cockney git – or something like that – to the game. But I still jumped up when we scored again. I didn't give in. I suppose it was friendly abuse really, because I'm still here to tell the story.

Chelsea is our name

I've been a Chelsea fan since I was a little boy.
Like so many people of my age, it all started when we
beat Leeds in the Cup Final replay. I was hooked
after that. They were the team then, especially Peter
Osgood, and they were certainly as glamorous then
as they are now.

I was brought up in Tooting and used to go down
the Bridge with a big gang of mates from school. My
first game was against Arsenal about 20 years ago,
perhaps even more, and I was pretty regular for
years after that. We didn't really get to that many
away games because it was so expensive to travel,
but we did make a special effort to get to the London
derbies. My parents used to worry about me going
but I was lucky enough to never see any trouble.
Well, at least I didn't get involved in it. I still go a lot
now, but I'm not seen because I go in disguise! Mind
you I had to come clean the other week because I
jumped up when we scored and forgot I had a cup of
hot tea in my hand. It went all over this woman next
to us and I ended up consoling her and giving £30 to
get her jacket cleaned. And I'd only just bought the
tea as well.

I was a Shed Boy for a bit when I was little but
I've never really had a favourite part of the ground.
Wherever you go at Stamford Bridge the atmosphere
is different class and I've always been into the
singing. It's sad that the loyal supporters are getting
priced out, but overall, we're in the best part of

London, we've got a great gaff and I think it's all coming together nicely.

I watched a lot of the games in the late seventies and that's probably when the team were at their worst. I wouldn't like to say who were the worst players were though. I don't want to depress the boys. I'm a fan who doesn't want to upset the players, old or new. They were bad times but you never thought about jacking it in and going to watch some other team. It was a long wait but looking at how things are going now, it was worth it because now we really are the best team in the world.

Snooker takes me all round the world nowadays and if I am out of the country, I manage to keep up with the results through various means, usually with the help of the press boys. My favourite piece of Chelsea memorabilia is the letters CFC moulded in lead. I brought it at a charity auction and now it's stuck on my snooker room door. It's absolutely brilliant. I spend a lot of time in that room practising, although perhaps not as much as I should. I'm probably going to get myself into trouble for saying this but I quite often used to go to Chelsea when I should have been playing snooker. I used to pretend I was practising but I was really in the Shed. So let's hope the wife never reads this.